The Callani

The cycle of the year celebrated in the sacred landscape of the Western Isles

Jill Smith

'There is .... on the island .... a notable temple which is spherical in shape .... the moon, as viewed from this island, appears to be but a little distance from the earth .... the God visits the island every 19 years and dances continuously the night through from the Vernal Equinox until the rising of the Plaeides....'

Diodorus of Sicily 55 BC
writing of the Hyperboreans.

The Callanish Dance

The cycle of the year celebrated in the sacred landscape of the Western Isles

©2000 Jill Smith

ISBN 186163 110 3

Photographs, diagrams and illustrations from original pastel artworks by Jill Smith
Cover illustration by Jill Smith
Cover design by Paul Mason

Published by:

Capall Bann Publishing
Freshfields
Chieveley
Berks
RG20 8TF

For Kevin, Tiffany, Saffron, Taliesin, Hazel and Alice
for they are the ones who come after;

for Phyllis and George, for they were the ones who went
before;

and for the Ancestors, for it was they who allowed my
journeys.

Acknowledgements

Where do I begin? So many people have helped and supported me through many journeys - including life's journey. I cannot name you all, but I thank everyone who has given so much to me over the years, and please forgive me if I do not mention you personally. A few people, though, have been of outstanding help, support and inspiration in many ways, especially at the most critical points in my life. To these I owe especial thanks:

Freda Bax; Mandy Fry (Amanda Roberts); Sylvia Isaacs (Scarlett); Jennifer and Jerry Perry; Sandra and Andy Bell; Karen With; Maggie Parks, Phil and Jem; Aida Birch and Terry Hetherington; Eveon Gaines and the people of Talley Valley; Helen Stapleton; Geoff Blundell; Lorye Keats Hopper: Jan and Munro Gold.

Lynne Wood; Keith Payne; John Sharkey; Monica Sjoo.

(at Callanish): the late Annie Macleod; Ishbel Smith; Mary Macleod.

Rita MacDonald; Michelle MacEwan; Claire Hewitt; Brian Larkman; Stella Joy, Tara and Shamus; John Lacey; Bernie and Jan Chandler; Richard Ford; Helen Rowson and Alfie; Wendy Spencer; Zam Walker; Donna Scott (Mackenzie); Colleen Heller Rosado; Julie Simpson-Moody.

For help, advice and encouragement with this book as well as inspiration:-
Philip Heselton; Simant Bostock; Lisa Tenzin-Dolma; Samapatti Neeraj; Kathy Jones and especially Jo and Jonathan Fryer.

Contents

Jill Smith's articles, poetry and drawings have appeared since the early '80's in many magazines, including:Pagan Parenting Network Newsletter; The Pipes of PAN; Wood and Water; Northern Earth; The Ley Hunter; From the Flames; Source; Dalraida; Celtic Connections; Avalon Magazine....

Most editions of the Weímoon Almanac have included some aspect of her work.

Her original art-work is available for exhibitions; her cards etc. for sale in shops and her slide shows/ poetry performances are available for bookings.

She is also willing to act as tour guide for parties visiting the Isles of Lewis and Harris. For further details please contact her through publication address.

Part One - The Long Road To The Isles

Chapter 1

Stepping Out

This is the story of one woman's journeying: through life, through the sacred landscapes of the British Isles and primarily the journey round the cycle of the years during a decade lived on the Island of Lewis in the Western Isles of Scotland.

To begin with I need to tell the story of the years that led up to my being on those incredible islands, for the earlier journeys are intertwined with what came later and, as time's circles turn, nothing is ever unrelated to what comes before or after.

This is a very personal story, my story, and I am Jill Smith.

I was born in London in 1942, in the middle of the war, in a quiet northern suburb; orphaned aged two by cancer claiming both my parents within months of each other, and brought up by my mother's ageing parents.

I had throughout my childhood the sense almost of being an alien, of not belonging to any group of people around me. Lost, lonely, filled with a sadness I could not define, I found solace only in natural things - sitting in trees, lying on my back in the grass gazing at the sky and the moving clouds; in the smell of burning autumn leaves; in the chill as summer ended and we shifted towards winter; in the excitement of "bonfire night"- decorating my cousins' garden with lamps in the trees, and in the fire itself, roaring into the dark night; in playing alone in the snow, with the stillness, the white and blue, the occasional solitary robin; in walks at night through quiet streets with silence, moonlight or the glistening of wet pavements; in long bicycle rides and picnics in the countryside that seemed so safe in those days; in solitary walks through the City of London - still full of bomb sites turned to rough carparks; in ecstatic treks on holiday cliff-tops, windswept with the sea crashing beside me - and in the extraordinary magical awakening and change that seemed to come with the first powerful burst of each spring.

For these were the only times I felt empowered, filled with an ecstasy I did not understand, which seemed to drive me towards a life I knew must exist somewhere which was so very different from the one I was living. In all other aspects of my life I was repressed, withdrawn, unable to relate to other people socially or to be in any way what I perceived to be a normal human being.

I yearned with unremitting focus from very early childhood to go into the Theatre. I would have loved to be an ice-skater, a ballerina, a singer, a showgirl; but these options didn't seem open to me, so I longed for the Theatre. It seemed only by stepping from my grey-brown life in the wings onto the glitter, glamour, colour and light of the stage could I rediscover and express that power, that ecstasy I had known from the elements and seasons, from the earth and the terrifying endlessness of sky and space beyond.

I left school when I was nearly sixteen, and after lots of unskilled jobs and many auditions, I finally got myself into the Royal Academy of Dramatic Art. Once there, it wasn't exactly what I'd expected, and the reality of the theatre and

8

show biz that I experienced at that time didn't seem to satisfy whatever it was I was searching for. I didn't feel I was destined for a life to be spent scrabbling for occasional small parts in obscure TV productions I just couldn't relate to. Somehow I needed to be much more in control, to be who I wanted to be and create my own dreams of my self - or some other "better" self.

During this hiccup of dissatisfaction, I was side-tracked. I lost the plot. I met the man who was later to be my husband and began to have his children. New dreams were dangled momentarily in front of me, then snatched almost immediately away. The sudden desperate longing for children was, I realised later, a need to create the brothers and sisters I'd never had, to be part of a family. To belong. I'd lost my dream of the Theatre and the dream of Family came instead. However, it was only much later, as I grew older and wiser that I began to rationalise and understand these things.

Instead of the wild and wonderful teens and twenties my peers were enjoying in the '60's, I lived an even lonelier life than ever, tucked away in the isolation of bedsits as an "unmarried mother" as we were called in those days.

All those years are another story - finally getting married, working as a cleaner on the other side of London while still trying to breast-feed my babies, spending seven years from dawn to dusk at market and social research and by the time I was 28 with 3 children, Kevin, Tiffany and Saffron, (and completely ignorant of Saturn Returns!) having totally lost sight of my Self, my path in life, how to get on any path at all, of what anything meant or how to satisfy this desperate need for that indefinable something that still screamed at me that it existed somewhere. I was pretty much in despair.

I'd done bits of performing work with my husband, Bruce Lacey, and his mates, the Alberts, over the years, but none of this really seemed 'me'. A change began to happen in the '70's as the world of the arts opened up to all sorts of possibilities. Working as a family in Community Arts as 'The Laceys' was a first glimmering as to how I could use my own creative talents. I'd been "good at art" at school, but my theatrical urges (I am a Leo) had put that in the shade. Married to a Royal College of Art silver medallist and whatever else, meant that I never dared put pencil to paper in all the years of my marriage, but I began designing and making costumes, painting strange things we used in community events and generally becoming more involved in the creative process.

A major breakthrough on many levels came in about 1974 when, now known as Jill Bruce, I was involved with my husband and his mates in a quite extraordinary theatrical production called "The Electric Element" which we put on at the Theatre Royal, Stratford East. It wasn't exactly critically acclaimed, being a fantasy in which every member of the cast wrote their own scene which was then strung together into a bizarre science fantasy tale. I wrote, made costumes, designed and painted sets and created my own dream role as 'the most beautiful woman in the Universe'!! appearing in a different guise in each scene. When I finally stepped in front of a ten foot high golden fan, clothed in a golden dress with an ornate shop window dummy wig on my head to declaim a grand speech, before descending a flight of steps to perform a kind of Fred Astaire and Ginger Rogers dance, I was actually doing something that changed the course of my life. I had found a passage in Apuleius' "The Golden Ass" which I slightly re-wrote and that was what I declaimed each night for several weeks. The speech was invoking the Goddess and though I didn't know it at the time, that is exactly what I did and what I called into my life.

After this production, my husband and I (sic) then decided to work on our own as a Performance Art duo, (Bruce Lacey and Jill Bruce or 'Galactic Theatre') and we began an intense

10

period of creativity together. At last it all came pouring out. I was making films, taking photographs and slides to use in performances, writing, creating roles and performance ideas, creating environments, designing and making costumes, working in a darkroom, being an administrator, applying for grants, doing the accounts, getting bookings, being a 'roadie' and touring Britain performing extraordinary multi-media science fantasy productions.

But there was still something missing.

I need to go back in time a bit - to what was then an isolated incident, but which I now recognise as an early beginning to what my life has been for the past twenty years.

In 1967, a couple of road and rail journeys from London to Cardiff had taken me for the first time through the ancient landscape of Wiltshire. It hit me like the proverbial ton of bricks. My education had taught me there was little before the Romans except primitive savages, and I knew of nothing from these prehistoric cultures except for Stonehenge.

To suddenly pass through a landscape littered with round barrows, long barrows, the incredible structure of Silbury Hill and to realise there were such places as the vast stone circle of Avebury, awoke something ancient within me I had never consciously touched before.

Firstly, the landscape seemed alive. It seemed as though the spirits of some ancient people, my ancestors, rose up from the earth and screamed at me that my education had been all wrong, that these people had had a wisdom and knowledge beyond anything we know now and that it was virtually my duty to acknowledge that and put the story straight, so to speak. The landscape of Wiltshire seemed vibrant and alive in a way I'd never previously experienced it.

We took our then two children on holiday in Wiltshire and Dorset and I was astonished by the Avebury complex and such places as the great earthwork of Maiden Castle, where I remember just lying in bliss between bank and ditch in what I later acknowledged to be a gigantic earth vulva. Maybe at that point, although it didn't begin to bear fruit for another decade, I had a kind of re-birth. A re-birth from the womb of the Earth my Mother.

At Avebury we walked up to Windmill Hill. Here also I had what seemed to be an extraordinary "memory". I use superlatives like 'extraordinary' because these experiences were very rare at that time in my life and quite unlike anything I'd previously known.

I seemed to be back in a time when the people of south Britain were nomadic, not settled farmers, and we travelled the tracks on the high ridges of the land and gathered here on this hill annually, rather like the traditional travelling people still do at Appleby in Cumbria. It was so real and so clear, as though I were someone who'd done it for generations. This time I was standing on the hill, the peak of our tribal lands, and gazing down at something strange going on. There below, others, strangers, people I didn't know, were erecting the great stones of Avebury's circle. I felt our land was being imposed on, invaded; that something was changing and I wasn't comfortable with it, no longer part of it. My people also built things - West Kennett was our place, but this was something very different.

There was nothing I could do with this experience at that time in my life, and it wasn't until nine years later in the drought-ridden summer of 1976 that the next stage in this journey began.

I was looking after my then 96 year old grandmother after she'd had a spell in hospital. I'd been an avid reader of science fiction in my teens, but life had been so busy since then that I'd read practically nothing at all for many years and had only just got back into reading books, including science fiction once again. It was my birthday and my son Kevin bought me John Michell's "*A View over Atlantis*", perhaps thinking it was of that genre, and I sat and read it as I watched on my grandmother's television Mary Caine talking about Katherine Maltwood and the Glastonbury terrestrial zodiac. Many astonishing things were happening to me at that time anyway - another explosion of change - and reading Michell's book and watching the programme seemed to open up doors to remembering inside me. It was as though there was all this ancient knowledge inside me, as though the memory of it had been anaesthetised and the anaesthetic was beginning to wear off and I was waking up to a wealth of knowledge I'd always had. My experience of the next ten years was as though I was emerging from the mud at the bottom of a pool, up through ever-clearing water and out into the sunshine above. Not a New Age climbing towards "the Light", but a shaking off of the mud of forgetting and clearing the ways to remembering. There was still a long way to go - and there still is, but it was beginning......

Our Science Fantasy performances had been becoming more alchemical and I'd been hungrily delving into realms of magic and the elements - and when we were invited to perform 'non-electrically' at the last Barsham Faire in Suffolk, it was as though pieces of a jigsaw were clicking into place faster almost than I could cope with.

Creativity now seemed to come from going into a sort of meditative process to see what I could discover within myself. I emerged with a series of cyclic ceremonies to be performed in a circle, celebrating the ancient elements of Air, Fire, Water and Earth; the seasons, the sun, all aspects of fertility, every cycle of nature and cosmos imaginable. I felt in touch with the magic and the power of the earth and something else was awakening in me. I felt at last that everything was coming together, pieces of some massive jigsaw of existence just dropping into place.

Over the next few years we performed an enormous amount of these so-called 'rituals' at many of the subsequent East Anglian Albion Faires, and at Art Centres, Festivals, Universities, Art Colleges etc. all over the land. The Albion Faires especially always had a theme, so I delved into this meditative place each time to find the form and shape and matter of the performance. It was like dipping into a huge mine of knowledge which I was re-discovering little by little - but the emergence grew faster and faster and more and more powerful. The performances were very spectacular and theatrical. As a Leo I came into my own in fire performances, with flaring torches, burning straw dragons and lions, walking fire mazes and spirals and wearing a headdress of roaring fire as I walked and danced around. The energy of the fertility rituals also became very powerful, allowing me to experience much that was very new to me, perhaps awakening my own dormant and frustrated sexuality. Physically I now had hair bleached almost white which I dyed vibrant colours to match the theme of each performance.

Within all this theatricality was much that was deeply serious and also profoundly real. I felt as though I were in touch with everything as part of a giant network or web. I became very dissatisfied with the way in which I was living my ordinary life - feeling the need to live more as people had done until fairly recently. I was shocked at the amount of quite basic knowledge of how to do things - make things, mend things, grow things, tend things - knowledge built up over thousands of years - which was being lost at an incredible rate in just this century. I became fearful of how we would no longer know how to survive were the substance of the modern world to crumble, which it so easily could.

The performances were like journeys. The finding of how to perform them was like a journey and I felt compelled to make physical journeys also - out into the landscape; to go to ancient sacred sites to celebrate the major points of the year - the solstices, equinoxes and 'Celtic' quarter-day festivals of Samhain, Imbolc, Beltane and Lammas; to go to sacred places to sit and watch the dawns; to visit many ancient sites I'd never before seen, to touch their energy and take some of it into myself, to meet them like people and to journey between them. We did much of this in an ex-GPO three ton truck. We celebrated the places and we documented it all and showed it in several major environmental exhibitions at galleries such as the Acme in Covent Garden and eventually, the Serpentine Gallery in Hyde Park. There were aspects of all this with which I felt at that time an indefinable discomfort, but it was all escalating so fast and we were on an Arts Council grant and this just was the context in which it was all able to happen. The performance part of me was satisfied for a while: the silent rituals developing in me expressive and almost balletic skills.

The first physical landscape journey we made was in 1977 - around the Glastonbury zodiac, which by then had called to me for a year. Although it was completed in four days and was quite a traumatic time for reasons nothing to do with the journey, I was fascinated by how we entered a different reality: the reality of the zodiac which was separate and apart from normal reality and yet still alongside it. It was a reality that was timeless, opening up the doors through time, so that the past was here in the present, and the circle had its own sacred reality with the energy of the elements of the zodiac signs manifesting very intensely. After this journey I wrote some poems about each sign. They make me cringe now, but it was a beginning and I put together a booklet of the poems with photos and other stuff from the journey - my first little landscape journey booklet.....

When Albion did a Moon Faire I had to go into the deep meditative space again. I went in deeper and more completely than ever, as I'd never previously really related to lunar energy, being a fiery solar Leo - but my moon is in Cancer and this part of me, at first unknowingly, I then began to explore. This was another major stage in my life journey. Maybe something in me as a woman became more complete. My woman-power, my woman-magic began to surface. I'd tried to survive in a man's world by being as good as a man, maybe even a bit like a man, but now I began to find that which was truly my woman-self, my spirituality, and to find my strength and power in that.

Chapter 2

Leaving London

In 1978 my grandmother died, aged 98. I suppose this freed me from the city of my birth, in which I'd grown to hate living, although I had touched a profound and sacred reality in the power places of it, especially in the ancient City of London. I still feel deeply connected to these places which seem to have an indestructible energy and magic untouched by everything that is negative about the modern life being carried on around them. I feel these places were there and recognised as sacred before the city and will be there when the city has gone. I hope that by then there will still be some humans left to revere these places once more who will be empowered by and strengthened by them. For all this, I still found trying to live an ordinary life in the modern city quite unbearable.

I had not realised that a half-share in the proceeds from the sale of my grandmother's house would actually enable me to buy somewhere to live out of London. It was a huge thing to realise I could get out of a trap life seemed to have got me into. We began to search for a house in East Anglia to be near the Albion Faires and the people we had got to know there. We had been drawn to that area years before and nearly moved there then, but as Londoners, had chickened out at the last minute. Now seemed the right time - now that there was something to belong to, to be part of at last. I often wonder how different things would have been had we had the courage to make that move all those years before.

At last we found one of the few remaining small farms still available for sale at a reasonable price. It had been an 11 acre farm owned by an old couple. A local farmer who owned land on either side initially bought it so that he could uproot and burn an old orchard and then be able to take his farming machinery from one field to another without having to go out into the road. In fact that made it one huge field. He then sold to us the two little cottages, outbuildings and about $1^1/_5$ acres of land.

We moved there in 1979. I soon realised it was not really the right part of East Anglia for me. It was too near Norwich and not near enough to the Waveney Valley where most people we knew lived. It was actually a big lesson in not following a dream without really sussing out what it would actually be like.

It was all such an enormous upheaval. I loved the houses, which had never had electricity. There was no running water - just a well out the back. I began to learn some of those lost skills - how to grow vegetables, tend animals, make bread, dye fabric, make wine, jam and pickles, use the food that grew around me - take water from the well and return the water from my own body to the earth; to use what the earth provided and return the vegetable waste back into the earth. I felt part of a cycle in a way I had never understood before; part of the earth in a very real way.

The fruit and the vegetables, the plants, the eggs, the goat's milk...all became the sacred materials I used in our cyclic performances, along with objects - pebbles, wood, plants, feathers etc. from the ancient sacred sites we still visited to celebrate the festivals of the Cycle of the Year. It was all becoming more and more intensely real.....

But I had two teenage daughters (my son stayed in London) and they wanted the telly and hair-dryers and the other paraphernalia of the modern world that I was rejecting. It was my dream, not theirs. One of them hadn't even wanted to leave London. They wanted electricity and running water, hot water, a proper toilet and a bath. The day the electricity first came to that house, I cried. Electric light (which I still hate, even though I've now taken it back into my life for a while) shone into corners and nooks and crannies that had never seen the light since the house was built.

I was growing closer to the land and farther from the family. It seemed the upheaval was going on in every atom of my being. The performances seemed to be acting as a self-initiation into an ancient mystery and my woman-self; and "The Goddess" was teaching me through sun and moon, through earth, trees, elements and all the turning cycles of which I was now so profoundly a part.

I became almost allergic to electricity - and to houses. I spent more and more time outside - couldn't stand the evenings round electric fire and TV, and I went to sleep at night outside under the goat shelter, lying on the earth, woken by the sunrise on this flat East Anglian land. I photographed a year's sunrises from one spot on that land - another kind of journey showing the sun's apparent movement across the horizon and back again, through seasons and growth of crops. I loved to stand there, knowing the sun would rise, with all the birds and animals who also knew and who would become silent and still just before that glorious and affirming moment. Years and much life later I still love my memory of that piece of land, the initiation I went through there, the trees I planted there, especially a hazel which is my tree in the Celtic tree calendar. Even though I now have no access to it and wouldn't want to return, it is still like a personal sacred site in some realm of my own time/space.

I began to feel I wanted to withdraw from the superficial theatricality of the performances. The reality and depth of the ritual and ceremony was so personal - between me and the energies I was dealing with - much of it wasn't really for public view.

More than anything I wanted to be alone with place, alone with the ancient sacred parts of the land which I now perceived as the body of my mother the Earth. I was her child and I was being taught at a rate I could barely comprehend. It was almost like a madness. I began to go off to these places, to spend time alone with them: Avebury; nights in West Kennett long barrow, acknowledging it as the vagina and womb of the Hag Mother and in a way, of myself; by Swallowhead Spring; on Windmill Hill's barrows... Over the next few years I slept out on the land in all weathers and temperatures. I learned to clothe myself in layer upon over-lapping layer. Without tent to sleep in I was swathed in sleeping bag, sheet of plastic and was in fact wrapped in the cold itself like a cocoon. I slept in snow and frost - tucked away in little invisible places, nurtured and protected by the earth and the sacred places themselves, nestling down like a child into the body of my mother. I learned that damp wool kept me warm as with the old Highlanders who used to wrap themselves in a wet plaid. I felt that to sleep in a tent was to cut myself off as much as were I in a house. I loved to open my eyes and see the stars and moon right above me.

I was deeply inspired by the books of Michael Dames - 'The Silbury Treasure' and 'The Avebury Cycle'. Whether or not they are totally factually correct, I believe he hit on the innate truth about the cycles enacted in sacred landscape. There is sacred landscape which is natural, self-created and known by the ancient people and there is sacred landscape maybe enhanced by the megalith builders as they began to farm and settle in places rather than roam the larger seasonal landscapes of the hunter-gatherers. I felt called to the different parts of Avebury to celebrate each point on the circle of the year. It seemed such a complete cyclic landscape in such a small area, and in Wiltshire I re-connected with those ancient ancestors who'd reached out to me in 1967. I think real teachings come not through words but from the places themselves which have the spirits of our ancestors still in them and those ancestors were themselves taught by place anyway. It was like some kind of direct transmission.

I think it is a profound insult to say that ancient people created myths and legends to explain away things they did not understand. As I see it these people evolved from the earth, sea, sun and moon and understood far more about them than we do and they were really present in the universe in a way that we are not and they had a real knowledge and a real truth. If these truths were then put into stories as a way of passing on the knowledge in a society that didn't write things down, then we are looking at things in the wrong way if we don't look at the truths in those stories. (For example in the book "Hamlet's Mill" Giorgio de Santillana explains how the ancients understood the precession of the equinoxes and the cycle of the Great Year). To call ancient people "primitive" just because they did not use writing and say they left nothing of their culture behind them is both insult and ignorance. It's amazing how much still does remain in British folk-tales and even in faerie stories. It just needs looking at from a different perspective.

One winter around this time I went every full and dark moon to a well or spring or a long barrow or chambered cairn. I slept at these places, stayed at them sometimes for days. Just being. Without expectation. Not hoping for phenomena. It was all phenomenal enough as it was. The cold and the small amount of food and water made it all like a vision quest I suppose. I've never felt the need for drugs - my brain seems to do incredible enough things as it is. The understanding comes later. There is knowledge which is without words - maybe knowledge which even early hominids had before they had speech. Maybe that incredible brain we seem to use so little of nowadays was about other ways of communicating than speech. Speech may help us in our daily lives; maybe it hinders our magical, spiritual and mystical communication. Maybe writing was another stage in losing it. If it's written, if it's printed, then you don't need to remember, to hold the stories and the songs of the land inside you, or to communicate with place, animals and other humans without words. Now there are computers and maybe even more of our original self is atrophying through mis-use.

As I've said, at this time at the beginning of the '80's I could hardly bear houses. I'd visit people and sleep in their garden. If I visited someone with no garden they said when I rolled out my sleeping bag it seemed to bring the forest floor and the faeries with it.

I began to feel that linking sacred places by the path of my walking was really important - that this was what the nomadic peoples had done - it was a way of tending the land, keeping it well and keeping the people well also. Not healing, just keeping well. Understanding the energies of both and acknowledging they are the same; that the people were the land and the land was the people. One being. It is what we have lost, why things are out of balance - in us - in the earth maybe - though I think ultimately the earth will be OK if we don't totally destroy her; but she may have to rid herself of us in order to be alright!

When I went to Australia in 1984, spending a month at Uluru (Ayers Rock) this was what the great teaching was. The Dreaming Paths and Song Lines of the People were what we once had too. They are still there if we will just sit and listen and be with and go where we feel we have to go. I think it is really important that some of us still do this. It is physical at the same time as being spiritual and perhaps even more important than some of the airy-fairy New Age all-in-the-head 'healing' which is around these days. "Touch the Earth", a book of Native American words popular in the '70's was called, and we who are of the earth still need to touch the earth, really touch the earth.

When I spent nights and days in long barrows and chambered cairns: Waylands Smithy, West Kennett, Grey Cairns of Camster - and many others, I seemed to 'remember' an aspect of what had been done there - that they were places of death and rebirth, not only of physical death where people were taken through something like the Tibetan Bardo, but the death and rebirth of shamanic initiation; home of the spirits of the ancestors, places of oracular prophesy.

I would often experience these things like personal memory, and I began to work them into poems. I was a prolific writer anyway, but I began the discipline of condensing wild words into a poetic form.

Chapter 3

Awakening to Callanish

In all the years of visiting ancient sites I had been very aware of the Callanish Stones on the Isle of Lewis in the Western Isles of Scotland, and felt very drawn there; but the circumstances of my life had not yet permitted me to go that far north.

I knew a group of artists, writers and photographers who had spent a lot of time at Callanish in the summers of '80 and '81, but it hadn't been the right time for me to join them.

In 1982 I realised this was the time I had to go. I could deny the call no longer, not only from Callanish itself, but from a mountain known as 'The Sleeping Beauty', who lies like a sleeping woman in the landscape of Lewis. I will tell more of her later. I had been told about her by some of these artists on their return, and she haunted my dreams and my waking hours, sometimes giving me visions of her from above as I seemed to fly over her like an eagle returning to its eyrie at her brow.

A group of people were going to meet at Callanish for the Summer Solstice of '82 and I felt at last I must be with them. I didn't feel I could just go there, like a tourist, like a casual visitor - it had to be a pilgrimage. Callanish had to be the goal at the end of a major journey.

So - I went to Lands End and began my journey to the Western Isles from there.

I had received Dzog Chen teachings from the Tibetan master Namkhai Norbu Rinpoche and had learned a practise of purification where one purifies a sequence of 'places' in one's body. These also represent many other things. I, and other people I knew then, see the land of Britain as the figure of a/the Goddess lying on her side in the sea: Lands End her feet, Wiltshire her genitals and so on - Wales maybe her pregnant belly and the far North of Scotland and the quartz crystal rocks of the Western Isles - her brow.

There seemed to be ancient sacred sites - stone circles - at various points on the body of the land which represented these 'places', so, as I travelled up the land I stopped at each of these ancient sites and carried out the purification practise. As I did so it seemed that these places in the body of the land were being integrated with the corresponding places in my own body and I and the land were becoming one. It was incredibly powerful.

I did not walk all the way - that is something I'd still love to do in the future - but got to within maybe 20 miles of each site and walked from there in a pilgrimage to each. Once there I'd stay a few days, sleeping in or near the stones, being with them all day, feeling totally part of the place, yet knowing all the time that pull ever Northwards and perceiving something like a line of light snaking up the land which seemed to be the path that I was following.

The sites were:

> Boscawen -Un, Cornwall................the feet
> Avebury, Wiltshire..........................the genitals
> Arbor Low, Derbyshire...................the navel
> Castlerigg, Cumbria.......................the heart
> Twelve Apostles, nr.Dumfries..........the throat
> Callanish, Isle of Lewis...................the brow

'Awakening' Journey - Lands End to Hebrides 1982

I also stopped a while at Glastonbury in Somerset, for this natural ancient sacred landscape, with its Tor, its hills, its wells - the Isle of Avalon - has always been a place where I pause on journeys; to look back on what I have done so far, re-assess what I am doing, re-focus and ground myself before I move on, because often the preparations for and beginning of a journey are wild and exciting and very busy in the urge to get started and there is a need for calm focus or else the point of the whole journey may be lost.

The Dumfries part of the journey was especially interesting as I'd not felt totally happy with the Twelve Apostles stone circle near Lincluden as the throat. I stayed around the area for days, going into the town each day, then walking out to a different nearby sacred site for each night. I had some intense experiences at some wonderful places until, on the last night, I finally reached an ancient well which I slept beside to the sounds of foxes cries and, I'm sure, of faeries, and where I seemed very close to the presence of a group of ancient ancestral 'grandmothers'. This, I felt sure, was the true throat of Albion.

I paused also on the lower slopes of Ben Nevis where I was ferociously bitten - quite some introduction to the dreaded Highland Midge!

I paused as though girding my loins in preparation for this first visit to the Hebridean Islands, which were so totally different from anything I had known in this life before, and which I seemed to have waited so very long, maybe lifetimes long, to meet.

I thought maybe I would journey slowly through Skye onto Harris and then up to Lewis, but once near the edge of mainland Britain, the urge to get to the Outer Isles was desperate and I travelled fast through Skye, feeling I must leave a proper meeting with this island until such time in the future when I was not so distracted and could give it my whole attention. Skye is the land of Scathac, the ancient warrior queen who taught the Irish hero Cu Chulain his warrior skills. She lies there still, I believe, in the Cuillin Mountains where, in later years, camping in wild storms, I had visions of wild harpies nesting in the mountain tops.

I stood waiting for the ferry at Uig on Skye with an anticipation and excitement I have rarely known, as I was about to embark on the almost last stage of this monumental journey.

As I crossed the Minch for the first time there were rainbows and visions of sky goddesses shining down their cloak-like rays. I felt I was being told that I was doing the right thing. I was on some path of inevitability, travelling on an energy beyond my control. Guided. Protected. But on the edge of something vast.

It was evening as the ferry pulled in to Tarbert on Harris. This was June and that far north the nights do not get dark. There is a magical twilight that simply grows to dawn again. It is like the realm of faerie. There were, however, lights twinkling in the harbour, and as I stepped off the ferry and walked up the hill to find myself a place to sleep on the heather-covered moor, I experienced something totally unexpected and completely overwhelming.

I had come home.

I had not known I was looking for anywhere, yet I had found something I hadn't even sought - or maybe it had found me. I had never felt so right anywhere, never felt so much that this was how things should be.

When I finally nestled down to sleep in a hollow in the peat, I felt the faerie-folk had prepared my bed for me.

Over the next few days I walked down the east side of South Harris to Rodel at the southerly tip. I watched the yellow irises growing beside still lochs whose edges slurped as though in conversation with the drinking water in the bottle I carried. I watched men turning the peats to dry - something I knew so little of then. I felt part of the stillness, part of the silence. I felt as though I were at the top of the world. There is something about reaching an island like this, especially at the end of a long journey. It is the end of the journey. There is nowhere else to go. The movement and energy of travel ceases. It is home. On the mainland almost everywhere is on the road to somewhere else. Here there is just the ocean, with only St.Kilda 40 miles to the West - and maybe the otherworld realm of Tir nan Og....

Tir nan Og feels very close here, especially on those magical summer nights.

After a few days I met up with two friends - John Sharkey and Keith Payne, who were travelling right up through the Western Isles and writing a book about it*, and with them, I began the last part of my journey to Callanish.

One afternoon I walked with them along a beach to an old chapel at Toe Head past Northton. I had never seen anywhere that seemed so untouched by humanity, that seemed so much like the earth had been before humanity existed and I knew I was going to live with this land. I didn't know how but I knew there was no way it would not be. There was an old stone wall, there were the remains of old lazy-beds - the hard-won strips of earth where the people used to grow their crops - there was a tiny bit of driftwood on the shore, but to my naive eye there were no other signs of civilisation. I walked along behind the men. Barefoot, I walked on the edge of the water, the tiny waves bathing my feet and washing my footprints away. The men walked in boots and left their bootprints in the sand.

29

On the morning of the day when I was finally going to see the Callanish Stones and the Sleeping Beauty Mountain for the first time, we paused one last time on West South Harris beside a lichen-covered megalith known as Clach Macleod. The stone felt like the personification of the energy that had carried me north and had protected and nurtured me throughout. I felt very emotional.

At last I reached Lewis and the goal of my journey. When I first saw the Sleeping Beauty mountain from Arivruach on the road from Harris to Lewis - lying there so alive, like one of the primal Creation giants, waiting to awake and walk the earth once more, I was almost overcome. Only a solitary tear crept down my cheek, but I was speechless. In these situations I cannot enthuse: "Gosh, wow, amazing, fantastic!", I am just silent with the enormity of something which I know has changed my life.

And then we were at Callanish, the Brow of Britain, with its stones of crystal, and the white, pink, black and grey of the Lewisian Gneiss which alters their colour and presence with each change of light, time of day, season or phase of moon.....but I was to find all that out much later over a period of many years...

Some days later a small group of us walked the length of the body of the Sleeping Beauty mountain. We were initially guided by someone who'd already made the journey several times (a man who claimed he could never resist a beautiful woman!), but I found that for parts of the journey I was almost blown along by the wind. We began at her feet - I was blown away from her vulva and onto her knees - along her belly, her breasts, her vast plain of a throat, past her chin and her great rocky nose (where there were indeed the remains of an eagle's eyrie) to finally reach her brow. Writer, artist and friend, Monica Sjöö had been part of the group to begin with, but she turned back after a while, feeling she could not trample on the body of our Mother; but I did not feel like this - I felt my footsteps were caressing Her, for I walked on her with love. It was the final moment of my great journey. I lay on Her brow, my brow to Her brow and it seemed that the journey that I'd made up the body of the land joined with the body of the mountain and my body as well. It was all one thing, all one body. That will be with me for ever.

The weeks I spent in the islands that summer of '82 were, as I keep saying, totally unlike anything of my life up to that point (or I now realise, since!). The energies and the emotions were explosive; everything was in upheaval, churned around, changed, not easy to deal with. It was such a height and depth of experience it was difficult to contemplate going back, going down to the 'ordinary-ness' of England, for it felt that life could never be the same again. The message from the stones and the landscape, which seemed to be coming through so powerfully from the ancestors, was not to seek externally for teachings, but to seek within, for we know it all already and all we need to do is re-member.

But I had to go back, and life wasn't ever the same again.

Some time later I wrote a story based on that '82 journey. I called it "Awakening" and wrote it in the third person. It was like a myth or a fable and so far I've only published it myself, but it stands up to time and someday I'd like to distribute it more widely. This was the end of a journey, if any journey can actually end, for I always say that the end of one journey is the beginning of the next and at that time it was very much the beginning of a new life.

Although '82 was a really wet summer in England - indeed overhead storms had followed me from stone circle to stone circle as I travelled up the land and I had sheltered under hedges and dried my clothes on them when the hot summer sun came out again and the farmers came round to count the cattle to check that none had been struck by lightning - in the islands, that summer had been exceptionally dry. I can still remember those nights, those days, sleeping in the heather, sitting watching the cotton grass wafting in the gentle breeze and listening to the magical sound of the snipe. It's part of me still and always will be.

I knew I was going to live there. It was already my real home. I went back there over and over and over at all times of year and in all weathers - camping out, sleeping in byres, being with this land that would not let me go. I ran back to it for comfort whenever life in England got unbearable. I'd stand on a quiet corner in a Suffolk village, stick out my magic thumb and 23 hours (my record) later I'd be sitting with a cup of tea in the Fisherman's Mission in Ullapool, (which was then one of my top ten Best British Caffs - it's gone now) waiting for the ferry to Stornoway on Lewis. Later I'd sit in Callanish village by the fireside of Annie Macleod, the 'wise woman of Callanish' who had such knowledge of the sacred sites of the islands, and her presence would heal me and then I'd go up the road - 'Peewit hill' - to stay with her sister Ishbel, sit by lamplight in a power-cut and she'd teach me of the practicalities of life on Lewis as she did in later years when I lived there.

There was something about that '82 journey that can never be repeated. I have learned so much since then, got a little wiser, a little calmer, and I can never again be in that almost child-like state, seeing and experiencing everything for the first time. For someone who'd lived most of her life in London, walking through the land from toe to brow, sleeping in the arms of the earth, my mother, was a primal initiation into the relationship of the human with the land which once we were all born to. A poet friend (male) said of me that year that it was like watching a butterfly emerge - "Bleedin' poet!" I muttered, but it really was like that.

When I returned, went back down, to England, my whole world blew apart. Doing that toe to brow journey and then being on Lewis; living out with the land all that time, I could not just return to life as I had lived it before. My family had been getting on better without me anyway; my beloved goat Sarny Sou had died the day I walked on the Sleeping Beauty mountain; I had maybe had a kind of breakdown from the stress of all the years of running a household with little money and administrating a business; I maybe at long last needed that time for myself that most people have in their teens and early 20's. It's an interesting observation that people giving me lifts when I was hitching often thought I was a student and asked what my parents thought about what I was doing! I was 40!

I certainly saw clearly that from my point of view, my marriage had actually broken down years before. I'd just been too busy to understand why I was often so unhappy. So it was with inner sadness and a sense of enormity that I left living with my two daughters, left the little cottages and outbuildings and the land with the flourishing hazel tree.

I drove in my old Morris 1000 van to the pub in Bungay, Suffolk where, after all the years of social isolation in my marriage, I had at last made a few friends and had people to turn to.

I ended up firstly in a borrowed caravan and later in my own (my first very own real home of my own) in a "small field in Kirby Cane". I was for a while free of all the possessions that had burdened me for so long, having little more than I could carry on my back. I had, after all the years of the responsibilty of motherhood, the freedom to go to places like Greenham Common and do anything, feeling that if I got arrested it didn't matter. I had a pause in life to just sit and listen to the birds in the trees, watch the light shining through them and take some sort of stock of my life. It wasn't a calm time: it was crazy, wild, mad and still very lonely. When you are suddenly free to do anything, the choices are terrifying, the worst one being the fear that you actually won't do any of them.

I started to write in a more organised way. I wrote my "Awakening" story and I started to structure poems I could be confident of reading in public. It took a lot of courage, but I started to do pastel drawings of what I experienced on journeys and at sacred sites. I hardly dared to make marks on the paper to begin with, for there was so much imagery in my head that I doubted my ability to convey it well enough on to the paper. Those early drawings, although tentative and pale, were so dynamic, so full of energy, quite different from the calm of much of my later work.

I continued the journeying and the time lived out with sacred sites. I visited Lewis again and again, finding sometimes my only real comfort with the Callanish stones and the sacred landscape there.

In the summer of '83 I went again to Callanish for the Summer Solstice and on from there round the little-travelled North-West corner of Scotland and along to John 'O Groats and over to Orkney on the little passenger ferry. I went over to the main island and spent about a week with the major Neolithic sites there. I didn't like the actual island of Orkney but I loved some of the sites, especially the Neolithic village of Skara Brae, buried for thousands of years by the sand and then fairly recently re-exposed. I seemed to relate to the community that once lived there. The furniture in the houses is made of stone and one building is shaped like the body of a woman/goddess and was, I think, a pottery, the kiln or oven being in the position of the womb. I spent several days there watching the tide go in and out and a man come and retrieve driftwood and pile it up to dry. All this time I was still without a tent and it rained the whole week! I wrapped myself securely in a sheet of plastic - once even on a camp-site - and managed not to get really wet. On the return boat journey I sat on deck and got drenched!

Throughout all this time in '83 I felt a very powerful presence with me, as though a companion was at my shoulder, already travelling with me; and a year later, in the summer of '84, when I was almost 42, after an agonising couple of years of apparent infertility, I gave birth to my fourth child, Taliesin. It was 15 years since I had had a baby and I had realised a lot of things in the intervening years about how I now believed babies should be spiritually nurtured in the womb, how the birth should be and how children should be reared in their early years. When it neared the time of his birth he seemed to take me right across Britain and into Wales to be born at the tipi valley near Talley. He was due on the dark moon when there was a solar eclipse, but decided to wait until the full moon, when, deep in the valley, surrounded on three sides by running water, my feet on the good earth and supported by some strong and trusted women, he finally came out into the light.

* *"The Road Through The Isles"* Wildwood. 1986.

Chapter 4

The Gipsy Switch

Shortly after his birth we set out again. The Gipsy Switch was a year-long journey round England and Wales. It had been given to me as a diagram a few years before and I'd carried the piece of paper with me everywhere, through all the upheavals and changes, for I knew I must travel it one day. It was like a wheel of the year with the hub at Arbor Low stone circle in Derbyshire. There were twelve named places corresponding to the 12 zodiac months of the year, so as one travelled one would be in each appropriate sign at the right time of year. This was a different kind of journey. It was a tracing of the movement of the skies, the cosmos, the turning zodiac wheel, upon the earth - macrocosm and microcosm turning as one.

I know very little of how much this was actually a traditional travelling route - a circle of horse fairs? - but it was what I had to do at that time in my life, the next move, the next journey, the next circle, the next cycle. It felt important as a way in which I would tune myself in as the human part of this great cosmic/earthly cycle. I feel that for a vast proportion of our time as human beings, that is what we did, that is what we were - the human link. We used to be born to it; we used to have it as our songs and stories and we knew them and travelled them before we could walk or talk, but now we have to find them again. This was part of my way of doing it.

I had met a lot of people on "The Walk for Life", which had gone from Faslane to Greenham Common in the summer of '83, and initially many of them were enthusiastic about the idea - to travel the Gipsy Switch journey in an old bus, performing 'Peace Theatre' on the way; but as time went by and the reality of a year's committment became apparent, the group dwindled and dwindled until it was very small. When we finally set off it was with two ponies, two flat-bed trolleys with hazel benders covered in tarpaulins, (mine was bright blue plastic!) a tent, two bikes, three adults, one baby and a few other people who came and went in varying permutations.

Preparing for the journey, in East Anglia, had shown me how apart I had grown from the old "Albion Faire" crowd. The old hippies of the '60's and '70's were fast becoming the affluent, fairly 'straight' middle-aged, middle class of Thatcher's Britain. I was involved with a group of much younger people now. Although I always insist I am not, and never have been, a 'hippie', whatever that actually means, I think people of my own age at that time were somehow challenged by the reality of what I was doing. Maybe it was just that they'd all done it all already. I hadn't done it when they did, so I was doing it now, but I felt very unsupported by most people I had thought were my friends in that area, and some were very negative and created serious problems for me. One learns life's lessons the hard way! However, other friends all over the land fed me such love and support it really didn't matter.

When marked on the map of Britain, the journey was more like an egg than a circle - an egg in the womb of Albion. Travelling west and north from Suffolk it took us quite a while to get to a point where we were actually on the 'wheel of the year' at a point fifteen miles south of Lincoln. The journey then travelled clockwise round Cambridgeshire (Libra), Essex (Scorpio), Kingston-on-Thames, (Sagittarius), Wiltshire (Capricorn), Glastonbury (Aquarius), Lampeter in West Wales (Pisces), Anglesey (Aries), Ireland (Taurus), Appleby in Cumbria (Gemini), Durham (Cancer), York (Leo) and back to Lincolnshire again for Virgo.

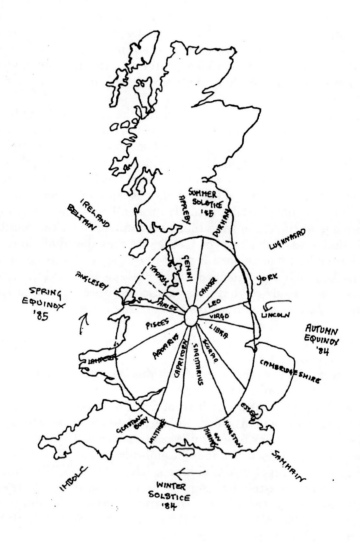

The Gipsy Switch

We began the journey when Taliesin was a few weeks old and ended when he was fourteen months. What a wonderful way to spend your first year of life!

In the early weeks the journey had its own momentum with various people travelling it, some all the time, others coming and going. Talie and I fully experienced the energy of Virgo for a few weeks and then went off for a while to fulfill something that had already been arranged. We went to Central Australia - so, as the others on the Gipsy Switch travelled the circle on the land of Britain, we travelled the circle round the Earth. It felt as though somehow we were still on the journey, still connected. This was the time of Libra and we celebrated the Spring Equinox in a cave in the great red rock of Uluru as the others celebrated the Autumn Equinox in Cambridgeshire in England. It felt like the complete Libra balance, and circles within circles within circles.

My understanding of so much was opened up by my time spent with the sacred landscape round Uluru and in the vicinity of the traditional People of that land. When I returned to Britain, soon after to visit the terrestrial zodiac of Kingston and later the zodiacs of Glastonbury and Lampeter, I was aware of the vital life and reality of these Dreamtime figures in our own landscape. My time in Australia also opened up the "doorways through time" in my awareness of my own ancestral past, as though I could see and feel back in time. There were teachings 'in the air' somehow, as though they could be tuned into like radio waves. The teachings were not like 'cultural rip-off', stealing esoteric knowledge from the People, but teachings of how to be aware of my own ancestry, my own spiritual history, my own sacred landscape. It is not a teaching of words, but a state of awareness, a way of seeing, that came as a kind of direct transmission. I didn't really say much about what I was experiencing. I couldn't while I was in it. From a very agitated mind-state I entered a very altered state of reality while I was near the rock. It was only on the last day there when my mind became busy again with worry about packing, travelling and the nightmare of the return flight to Britain, that I realised how different everything had been.

I am very grateful for that experience at that time in my life and to my friend Lynne Wood who looked after me on many levels and put up with quite a lot.

We returned to the late Autumn in England, meeting up with the others at the Saffron Walden maze in Essex, in Scorpio, in a world of rich gold autumn colours. My waggon had been somewhat invaded by mice (!) who had gnawed their way through some costumes, but otherwise everything was as I had left it and I felt rather guilty that Richard Ford, who's home it had become, now had to move into a tent. Thank you for looking after everything so well, Richard.

We had a hard, cold winter in Wiltshire and Somerset, my baby being incredibly big and bouncy, healthy and cosy, swathed in layers of woolies, but I got very neurotic about keeping the place warm, it being very difficult to find Calor Gas cylinders and paraffin which I used for heating. By this time it was usually only me and the baby and one other person travelling. These were young men and they did not understand the priorities and responsibilities I had with a young baby and they found me difficult and the situation got very stressful at times. I suppose it was all so different from how it had started out, with a lot of people on the journey to do all the work that needed to be done.

When we got to Lampeter in West Wales, for various reasons, all the others decided they didn't want to go any further. For me, the journey, the circle on the land, being in the right place at the right time, was the most important thing. I had to carry on, but I couldn't cope with a pony, a large trolley and a baby on my own. I needed to walk. Everything fell into place like magic. Someone wanted to buy my pony and arranged a means for her to travel back to East Anglia. The people I was staying with in Lampeter wanted to buy the trolley. I had somewhere to store all the gear I had in the waggon. It took a while to organise the practicalities, but I spent time in Anglesey in Aries and then returned through there on my way to Ireland where Talie and I spent Taurus on the mound of Tara in County Meath. We returned to England and got ourselves to Cumbria and then I walked for $3\frac{1}{2}$ months. I carried Talie in a 'Snugli' on my front, a huge rucksack on my back and a carrier bag in each hand. I got to Appleby in time for the Fair, where I was recognised by Gipsies from Essex and had to explain I hadn't got my horses with me any more. I walked across the spine of Albion, to Durham, down to York and then down to Lincoln and fifteen miles further south to where the journey had first touched the 'circle' a year before.

Travelling at our own pace without anyone else to have to fit in with, this was one of the most wonderful times of my whole life. I felt empowered and in control - a control that was part of nature, my ancestors and my mother the earth - as I had been at Talie's birth. This first year of his life was so wonderful, just moving through the land. What need for bright-coloured plastic toys when you have sticks and stones, grass and puddles and the sunrise in your waking eyes? He was so happy, so content, so calm, and he kept me laughing."How did you carry all the stuff you need for a baby?" people ask - but what do you need? Two good breasts, enough to drink, a change of clothes, a shop for food every couple of days, a bigger shop for nappies every couple of weeks and a little stove to heat a bit of water. Everything else people say you need is just marketing and exploitation. I now had a small but good quality tent and a warm and cosy sleeping bag. I learned the art of not carrying anything you don't need. I didn't carry a single scrap of paper I didn't need. I got rid of packaging, expelled even the air from packets of baby food and crammed individual nappies into every crevice of my rucksack. The only problem was finding places to get rid of rubbish. Lay-bys would have notices saying 'Please take your litter home', but this was my home. I sometimes walked for days with very heavy bags full of wet nappies until I found a rubbish bin. Not easy. I washed clothes whenever I had access to hot water, even in public toilets, and tied the wet washing on the rucksack to dry in the sun and wind.

I had rarely known such simple, straightforward joy as I did during those months. The winter part of the journey had been fraught with anxiety, so the summer came as such a relief. I seemed to be filling in more and more of my internal 'map of the land' - amazed at how you can still find small quiet roads to walk between cities, and having my faith in human nature restored by the incredible kindness shown us by all sorts of different people along the way, including an immense amount of help and advice from the traditional travelling people both when we were with the horses and even when I walked alone.

At the end of the journey I found myself in a field where the others had been the previous year when I was in Australia. Richard Ford with Juliet Yelverton and their baby Sharma, came to meet us and we went off to an ancient earthwork to celebrate this low-key conclusion to such an epic. I would have loved to walk into a town with banners waving, bands playing and crowds cheering, but the triumph turned almost into an anti-climax. The energy changed very quickly. Suddenly I was back in the 'real' world. For the whole time I'd travelled the Gipsy Switch, the journey was my home; where I slept each night was my home; each path I walked by day was my home. Suddenly, the journey was over and I was homeless. My possessions were scattered in peoples' attics - the object of some mirth to my 'friends' in Suffolk who were all fast turning into ageing 'yuppies' - and no-one there had offered me a home when I returned. Someone had 'caravan-sat' my old home in another field, but they wanted rid of it. The original "small field" had been deemed over-crowded by the local council when several other caravans had liked what I had there and come to join me.

In a kind of panic, suddenly feeling I had more than I could carry, after a lift to Nottingham, I boarded a hot over-crowded National Express coach on an August Bank Holiday and ran for the only place on Earth that felt like home. I took Talie for the first time to Callanish. My joy when I watched him crawl and play in our old camping place there was beyond imagination. To re-cap, this was the summer of 1985. The full moon changed the weather and the non-stop rain crept higher and higher in our tent. Our friend Ishbel told a young woman, Mary, who lived in a new house nearby, that we were there and Mary took us into her home for the weekend.

By now I was divorced and had reclaimed some of the money I'd put into the purchase of the house in Norfolk. I'd lived on some of it, so there wasn't all that much left, but there was still enough to buy some old place on Lewis. I tried to sound out Mary's relatives as to how they felt about English 'incomers' and they were very encouraging. On the day when I left to return to England I knew I had made my decision. It wasn't a dream or a fantasy. Talie and I really were going to live on Lewis. It was the only place that could be home.

The only person who had offered us a place to stay was Monica Sjöö, so we went to spend the winter in South West Wales where she was living. It was the time of terrible tragedy for Monica: her son Leif was killed in a road accident in France and her eldest son Sean was diagnosed with cancer.

Somehow I managed to sit in a tipi in her front garden and from a year's diaries I extracted writings of the Gipsy Switch to go on the walls of an exhibition I was about to have in a London gallery. Although I'd had a camera with me, this had been more for 'happy snaps' and recording Talie growing than for documenting the journey. I'd done so much photography

43

and documentation in the past that I felt there was a danger of seeing the world through the eye of a camera and I wanted to be right there in it with nothing between me and the world and to be able to communicate my experiences through my drawings. Staying in a room in London, I had 14 days before the exhibition opened to do 12 drawings from a whole year. With a $1^{1}/_{2}$ year old child and getting really ill in the middle of the fortnight, I was very satisfied with the discipline I achieved. In the day I did all the purchasing of materials, photocopying etc. etc. I needed, then every evening when Talie was asleep I did a picture, and at that point in my 'artistry' was pretty satisfied with what I created.

I then had an exhibition, with several performances, with my Australian friend Lynne Wood and her powerful work.

In February '86, accompanied by a friend, Val, who came to help with Talie, I travelled back to Lewis, rented a flat and hired a car for a week and went to look at everything that was for sale in my price-range. I had a week and I had to find somewhere in a week. The first couple of days left me pretty despondent. The North-West of Lewis didn't feel like the land I'd fallen in love with. (I know better now!) The only houses available were huge and grey and needed a lot of work done with improvement grants. There was nowhere I could afford available for sale in Callanish village. I couldn't face camping out for years in the garden of a house that was being pulled down and re-built. I needed somewhere I could move into and live in straight away.

The nights were frozen, there was a covering of snow, but the days were brilliant with hot sun and vibrant blue skies. On the third day we went to the area of Pairc or South Lochs, where I'd never been before. In previous houses we'd viewed, Talie hadn't even wanted to be put down onto the floor, but we parked in the township of Gravir and he toddled down the road singing, and when we went into the old corrugated iron

Church of Scotland Mission House and Hall - now called Tigh-a-Ghlinne, or House of the Glen, he ran round the sunshine-filled rooms, bursting with joy and I knew we had found our home.

South Lochs is all rocky hills, more like Harris than most of flat Lewis, and very beautiful, full of sea-lochs - though they ruined the journey into it during the years I lived there by a relentless programme of road-building that ended up like the motorway to nowhere, enabling a handful of people to get to Stornoway 10 minutes sooner - but I digress...

It wasn't that easy getting the place. The Lewis solicitors treated me - as an English woman living in Wales - very unfairly, but it was meant to be ours and when a closing date was set on offers it was mine that was accepted by the Church of Scotland - who remained for the next ten years my feudal overlords!

On Taliesin's 2nd birthday on the 13th June 1986, Tigh-a-Ghlinne became ours and, with a hired Luton van and the help of my younger daughter Saffron, I drove through Wales, across the South and East of England, collecting my bin-bags and cardboard boxes of precious remaining possessions, into Scotland, up to Ullapool, onto the Stornoway ferry and finally along the then narrow, winding and often precipitous road to the corrugated metal house full of sunshine that was to be ours through all the ups and downs of the next decade.

We had come home.

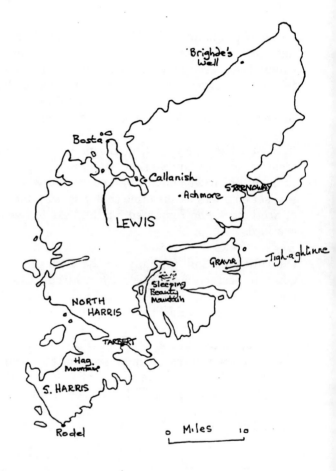

Brighde's
Well

Bosta

Callanish

STORNOWAY

Achmore

LEWIS

GRAVIR

Tigh-aghtinne

Sleeping
Beauty
Mountain

NORTH
HARRIS

TARBERT

Hag.
Mountain

S. HARRIS

Rodel

0 Miles 10

A Rough Map of Lowis and Harris

A rough map of Lewis and Harris

Chapter 5

Lewis - Setting the Scene

Writing this in 1998, 1986 seems an awful long time ago. A lifetime ago.

I had pursued with desperation this one goal, the only thing that seemed possible in my life - to buy my own house, however dilapidated, on my beloved Isle of Lewis, and make a life there; to let my little boy grow up and run around in the freedom of that land - the freedom also to do what he liked in our own house after years of being in and out of other people's. It was a reaction too, I suppose, to the years I had lived alone with my first little boy all those years before - in bedsits where I was told off if he made the slightest noise, where he couldn't behave naturally or in any sort of relaxed way. I wanted to close my own front door and be accountable to no-one. I needed to make my own decisions, no matter what anyone else thought of them, for I knew what my own priorities were and what was important for me at any one time. I wanted to be queen of my own castle. In all the years of my marriage I had never had even a shared bedroom, let alone my own room. I never had anywhere to escape to, apart from a dark-room or a cupboard under the stairs. I think at this time I was desperate for my "own space".

Once I was there, I immediately became frightened by the responsibility of the house. Although habitable by my standards, it would take a large part of each summer just patching and painting the roof and walls and trying to do some sort of repair to the window-frames. My two daughters, Tiffany and Saffron, came up that first summer and painted nearly the whole of the outside of the house in a week, to set

"Tigh-a-Ghlinne", Gravir, Isle of Lewis

me up for the winter, but after that I was on my own. I had little money left to pay people to do repairs that I could not do myself, and this I kept for real emergencies. It was a strange ambiguity that that which was my haven, my retreat, was also the source of much stress and, indeed, fear.

Having more or less lived outdoors for the previous 5 or 6 years, this house was like a mansion to me. At that point I do not think I could have lived in a 'proper' house, but this was like a half-and-half - a degree of compromise I could deal with. It was large. The front of the building was 19 metres long. It was all on one floor with an enormous attic over the house part. The hall, which had been the church, was as big as the house. This once had been accessible from the house, but the connecting door was now walled up, and I had to go out in all weathers and half way round the building to get into it. The whole building was entirely made of corrugated metal on a wooden frame, with no solid walls. Most of the roof had a cladding of wood underneath, being truly beautiful in the hall. The house had four rooms, a bathroom and a little scullery. The plumbing had long since deteriorated, pipes being bent back and closed off, presumably when there were bursts. The interior walls were either of ancient thin plasterboard, plywood or hardboard. It was unique and quite wonderful.

At first I slipped back into 'house' mode and got all the forms from the Hydro (Scottish Hydro-Electric) to have the electric put back on, but I stopped and thought "Why do I want electricity? I don't need it. I don't even like it!", so I decided to do without it. Although the place would probably have had to be re-wired, it wasn't so much a question of cost at that point - it was a conscious decision to live without electricity. That was what my life on that island was to be.

That far north there aren't the same seasons as in South England. The changes in the vegetation and landscape are very subtle. There are few trees, so there isn't that familiar cycle. There is nothing now grown in the way of crops. The Islands are in the Gulf Stream Drift, so the winters are comparatively warm (compared to mainland Scotland) though very wet and windy, and there is not that much variation in temperature between winter and summer. What does change - is the light.

The winters are long and the hours of daylight short, but the reward for enduring that is the incredible light of summer. During the two summer months from mid-May to mid-July, it doesn't get dark. The sun does set, but only just below the horizon, and the light remains as an almost unbelievably magical twilight. Everything that was difficult about living there seemed worth it for that wonderful, crazy, but amazingly healing time of summer.

What changed dramatically also, was the moon, who's movements are even more extreme that far north. The summer full moons hang low, barely rising above the hillside opposite the house; the winter full moons are unbelievably high, the light more powerful than I'd ever known it before, seeming to sear through the fabric of the building as though it were not there, and I would lie in my bed, bathed in moonlight as though I were outdoors. I have rarely felt so involved with the moon as I was on Lewis.The winter night skies were so dark and when clear, the stars were more brilliant than I had ever known them. Just think - this is how it was everywhere once.

So I realised that what I was doing was living the cycle of dark and light. These were the rhythms with which we evolved, yet nowadays increasingly, although we know when it is summer or winter, we come indoors in winter, switch on the lights, close the curtains, put on the telly and it's all the same. The reality of what's outside is shut out, denied, although it is an essential part of what we are.

We lived with candles, firelight, hurricane lamps and a tall chimneyed oil lamp. I don't even like Tilley lamps. I find their light, though brighter, cold, and they hiss and they are complicated to start, especially in the dark! I learned to walk around and do an awful lot of things with a torch tucked in my armpit. I had already learned to live very safely with fire and candles and Talie grew up with that knowledge.

At first I used an old Rayburn to warm one room, but it had already had its boiler removed so there was no hot water, and it was very inefficient. I used to huddle by its open door of an evening and then it would go out. It never got hot enough to cook much on. I did learn to get a pot of stew simmering for when I got back from the peats and we did once or twice bake bread, but that was a whole day's work requiring my full attention. Eventually too many bits of it rusted off for it to be safe and we moved into the "middle" room which had an open fireplace.

We burned the peat I spent all summer cutting. (When I wasn't on the roof or at Callanish!) Peat is a beautiful fuel and makes a lovely fire. It doesn't burn away as fast as wood and doesn't give off the horrible fumes of coal. Outside, walking the dark street through a township, the beautiful sweet smell of the peat smoke - the 'peat-reek' - was one of the things I had fallen in love with when I first went up there.

The down side is the incredible amount of fine ash it produces. This is lovely and soft and the most amazing range of colours, from white and grey through every conceivable hue of yellow and orange to a deep russet red - like a paleolithic cave-painter's palette - but it gets everywhere and when you clear the hearth it rises in a cloud and settles all over everything in the room. Of course I didn't have a vacuum cleaner to get rid of it all. It's now 2 years since I left and I still occasionally come across some possession covered in it. A little is good for the earth if you're growing things, but not too much. So I was told. Outside where there was a huge heap, it grew mosses and some beautiful wild plants.

I had to resort to a Calor Gas cooker and to Calor Gas heaters to heat the bedroom or the living room on summer evenings when it got chilly but wasn't worth lighting a fire. We often used a bedroom as a kind of bed-sit for a lot of the day. I think people watching my chimney thought I stayed in bed half the day! There was no delivery service for gas cylinders until just before I left and I found the whole procedure for getting gas extremely stressful.

After a few years I learned how to keep the fire in at night so that there was a warm room for the morning and a new fire rarely had to be lit. Most households up there keep a fire going throughout the year. I used to let the fire die down a bit, but not too much and then completely cover it in a mixture of crumbly bits of wet peat and earth which was pretty much peat anyway, and it would smoulder away all night and in the morning there'd be a deep bed of hot ash and if I put smallish fibrous bits of peat into it, it would soon burn up. With a few exceptions no-one ever showed me how to do very much: it was mostly a process of trial and error.

I thought nothing of boiling all my water for the washing and all the other things you need hot water for. I still do all my washing by hand. It was a sort of ritual that went on throughout the day, kettle-ful by kettle-ful. The washing dried easily in the Hebridean winds which blew most of the creases out, so I didn't really need an iron. It was only a few modern fabrics that seemed to get badly creased, so I avoided them wherever possible. We didn't have a bath, but we washed a lot. We may have looked a bit rough and ready, but we were basically clean.

So many aspects of how I lived were for positive reasons - actively chosen as a way of life I believed in. Although I could drive, I'd been walking the land for several years and initially there was no way I wanted to own a vehicle, burn petrol, pollute the atmosphere, so I was determined to travel by bus and to hitch. I'd rarely have problems getting anywhere hitching and it is completely safe on the islands.

After 4 years of doing this, I gave in.

My life there had by then changed somewhat; I'd become very dis-empowered and some of my priorities had shifted a bit. With financial help from an old friend I bought an aged Vauxhall Chevette estate which lasted me almost until I left the island. The sea air and salt on the winter roads wrought havoc with the body-work and the worry of 'would it start' and 'what's going to go wrong next?' caused me probably almost as much stress as it solved problems, but it gave me back some control of my life, for I had by then on a day to day level thought I was losing it all.

I believe totally in re-cycling and re-using. I rarely buy new things and this isn't entirely because of lack of money, but because I believe in not throwing things away, in prolonging the life of things until the last possible moment. I bought or was given mainly second-hand clothes - I think you actually end up with better quality stuff second-hand than buying cheap stuff new when you aren't well-off.

I had lived so many years in a state of anxiety over possessions and had rid myself of most of them. It was as though when I was younger I had to have possessions to prove I existed, to prove who or what I was - and I no longer needed that. I think I was happiest when I could carry all I owned, so I was determined that I would only accumulate old furniture that I wouldn't get attatched to and could just walk away from. I didn't want living on Lewis to become a trap. I wanted to feel that if I really needed to I could pack up the essentials and go. At the beginning I thought - "However little money I have I will always make sure I have the ferry fare in my pocket".

When I left my other family; when I left the work I did with my husband and all the stuff that went with it, in a way I left a whole identity, certainly a whole public identity. In the years since, I had built up another public identity, but these things have a way of becoming somewhat mythological and where was I really in the midst of it all? On Lewis it all counted for nothing. I think initially I was quite lost. I walked away from much more of my self than I should have and after a few years I realised I had to allow a lot more of my old self back in again.

I didn't really have plans for how I would live on Lewis, but I had ideas. The hall of the building was a beautiful place - big, calm and peaceful. I thought I would hold events there; performances maybe, music maybe - it seemed to have so much potential. I thought that I would pick up some aspect of the life I had lived when I was married, but everything was so completely different on Lewis and people's attitudes to me so very different from how they'd ever been before, that things never were as I'd expected. I did however turn the hall into a beautiful exhibition space. In the early years I exhibited work about Callanish and other aspects of the islands by myself and many other artists I knew, but later, as I produced more and better work myself, I had an annual exhibition of my own pictures, to which I had a trickle of valiant visitors from all over the world. I wasn't at Callanish. I wasn't on the 'tourist trail', but they made the long journey to this far corner of the Western Isles.
To the edge.

I had always been a knitter, had knitted almost as a form of meditation. I was fascinated by the traditional Fisherman's Gansey patterns, which are similar to, but different from, Aran knitting. Many of these echoed the patterns of Neolithic carvings and I thought I would research them and knit them. I even thought maybe I'd keep a couple of sheep out the back, shear them, dye their wool with traditional natural dyes, follow the whole process through and knit things from the wool. I did start by making 'knitted journeys' from wool picked up by the roadside which had been dropped by sheep before they were shorn. They do that a lot, especially if they aren't fed properly through the winter. But in all the years I lived there I knitted very little - less than in all my previous life, and this particular dream came to nothing. By the time I moved, the 'knitted journeys' and lots of un-knitted yarn, had gone to the moth and I buried them in the earth hoping they would make the Great Return.

I come from a basket-making family. My grand-father and great-grandfather had made industrial basketware in the City of London. In East Anglia I had started to learn from the apprentice of one of Norfolk's basket-making 'old boys'. I was fascinated by how completely differently Hebridean baskets were made from the English ones. English ones start at the bottom and work up, Hebridean ones work on a frame and start at the top and work to the bottom. I wanted to learn how to make and perhaps produce the traditional peat-creels, but as with so much on the Islands, the baby has been thrown out with the bath-water and no-one remains with the knowledge of how to make them. I never got it together. There is a man now, Alisdair Davidson from Arran, who has leant the skills and who makes them and teaches. I still want to learn.

In the early years, my failure to carry out these dreams did in fact seem to me to be just that - failure. It took me perhaps almost until I left to see and acknowledge what I had actually achieved during all those years. I am undyingly grateful to those few people on the island who believed in me. Most of my support came from people on the mainland, in England, even on the other side of the Earth, who had a more rounded view of what I was doing, but I only had occasional contact with them and they weren't there on a day-to-day basis. I was very much on my own.

I suppose when I moved there I had a somewhat romantic idea of the Islanders. I was quite in awe of them and didn't really challenge or confront them as I might people in England. I was fascinated by a way of life they had only just given up, indeed got rid of. It took me years to realise that there were aspects of it of which they almost felt ashamed and of which they couldn't see the strengths; strengths that can seem so obvious to outsiders, and on which they had now almost completely turned their backs. However, to criticise them for this is not allowed! The people had lived a very hard life. Until the Crofting Act (1886) they had been totally at the mercy of the land-owners and the tacksman and were often cruelly and inhumanly treated. It is difficult when suddenly your fortunes change to see what was good about a way of life that seemed so hard and impoverished.

Looking at it from the outside I think the traditional Black House of the Highlands and Islands was a perfect dwelling, indeed recent research has actually proved that to be so. The buildings were low, with very thick double walls. They nestled into the landscape in a both practical and aesthetically pleasing way. They withstood the storms and hurricanes. They had the fire in the centre of the main room and that was the heart of home and family. There was no chimney and the smoke went out through the thatched roof. The thatch was changed annually by the men while the women and children went up with the animals to the high pastures for the summer shielings, where they lived in tiny dwellings, once made of turf, more recently of wood and corrugated metal like my house. They made the butter and cheese for the winter from the plentiful summer milk and lived a carefree outdoor life that most look back on with nostalgia. This practise died out in about the 1930's. During this time the inner layer of soot-filled thatch from the black houses was put on the land as fertiliser and the outer layer put back on as the inner, with new thatch on the outside.

The meagre earth was built up into raised strips known as lazy-beds, which were also fertilised with sea-weed. They used every conceivable patch of cultivable land, even at quite precarious angles down steep gradients, the strips bending at curvy angles so that the growing crops would support each other against the wind. They grew what they needed for themselves and their few animals. There were few trees, so no wood for building and they were highly skilled at making roofs from driftwood and bits of old ships and furniture from fish-boxes.

The house and byre for the animals in winter was all under one roof - the heat from the animals helping to keep the household warm. In the winter they sat on either side of the fire having a ceilidh of local gossip and ancient lore, with the sleepy children listening and learning; working as they did so at the chores, mending nets and making clothes. The women knitted ceaselessly even when walking barefoot across the moor with a load of peats on their back. In the summer they worked outside, spinning and waulking (shrinking) the newly-woven cloth of the Harris tweed.

Having lived there 10 years I know now it is terribly important not to romanticise this way of life and to realise how hard it was, but it saddens me to see how totally they seem now to reject it. They live in very modern houses perched in inappropriate places, increasingly heated by oil-fired central heating; run new and flashy vehicles and do little with their land but keep heavily subsidised sheep. There is a problem in Stornoway with some of the young people who have lost their traditional way of life, yet do not feel themselves to be truly part of the modern world which they see in the media. One of the few traditions still continued is the weaving of the Harris tweed - the clickety-clack from the weaving sheds often being the only sound for miles on still evenings.

Naively I had hoped they would understand and support the way I had chosen to live, but realised later they looked down on me and tend to regard English incomers who come to live in an environmentally friendly way, grow their own vegetables etc. as a joke that won't last long.

I dug with great difficulty small areas of earth from the dense grass on our patch of land and grew a few vegetables. Although we had 1/4 acre, it was mostly rock and bog, full of deep ditches to divert the rain-water away from the house. It grew reeds and moss and thick grass, but very little of it had any depth of soil. It was also on quite a steep slope. I could grow enough potatoes to get us through the winter, and wonderful carrots. I could grow splendid broccoli too, for I needed fresh greens, but inevitably, just when it was ready, the sheep got in and destroyed it in a few minutes flat, for it was increasingly difficult to keep out a particular dynasty of Gravir sheep that could jump the highest fence. Friends from England would visit and say they were surprised I'd not done more with the garden, but my time in the summer was almost entirely taken up with painting and mending the roof and the whole process of turfing, cutting and drying the peats, carrying them from the banks to the road and then getting them home. This was traditionally a communal activity - everyone taking it in turns to do everyone elses and is often an extended family activity, those living off the island coming over for holidays to do the peats. It doesn't take so long when a whole gang does it, but I was just me on my own, working a few hours almost every day from April to September. Some years I did get bits of help from various people, but it was mainly...just me.

Gravir itself is a crofting township. There are no villages as in England, with a centre, a heart, a local pub or cafe where people gather, or a small group of shops. Crofts, which are strips or areas of land, are strung out along roads, round lochs etc., each with a succession of ruined or derelict houses of various ages and one or more modern ones currently inhabited (or, as in areas like South Lochs, increasingly used as holiday homes). To an English person the numbering of the houses is crazy, here there and everywhere - logical when you know the history of the crofts and families, but not when you just turn up unfamiliar with it all looking for a specific address. If you ask directions, people just want to know who you're looking for, very often not knowing the house numbers.

The heart of the township is the Church, where I expect all the gossip is exchanged and if you're not part of the Church, you're really outside of everything. The Free Church of Scotland is a very severe form of Presbyterianism. Not exactly my cup of tea.

Gravir sits round a long, deep sea-loch, like a Norwegian fjord. The river that feeds the loch goes inland to what is virtually the feet of the Sleeping Beauty, so although I couldn't see her from my house, I knew she was there and I saw her changing shape every time I went on the bus or drove to Stornoway to do my shopping. We looked up the Glen and I could see the changing weather coming. The predominant winds funnelled along the Glen and were South Westerlies coming straight at the end of the house. I realised after a few years that the house was built against the wind. No windows faced it and even the doors opened against it. It is a strong house, built to be their church nearly 100 years ago and it will last a long while yet. They used to tell me that, and I should not have been so fearful of the hurricanes that hit it. It stood firm when even prestigious modern buildings lost their roofs.

The houses are quite spaced apart - initially my nearest neighbours were hundreds of yards away and there were hills which prevented me seeing the dozens of houses strung out along both sides of the loch. I felt very relaxed and private. In later years more houses were built nearer to me and I began to feel more enclosed. The most recent part of Gravir - council scheme, school and doctor's surgery etc, was round a corner, hidden by another hill. I could see the Free Church from my house, and the congregation went past four times each Sunday on their way to and fro. Initially I felt very oppressed by the Sabbath - not being able to do anything outside, work on the house or at the peats, or even hang the washing out - even if it were the only fine day of the week, but in later years, as it became the day I created my pastel art-works, I came to value it as the day I didn't feel I 'had' to do things. Now in England, I still keep to this routine, but am filled with wicked glee as I hang out a line of laundry on the Sabbath!

We faced the hill opposite, which was the other side of the glen, and along there was the steep, curving road which led to my peat banks - a walk of perhaps $\frac{1}{4}$ mile from our house.

We lived 25 miles from Stornoway, the only town. We lived 30 miles from Callanish, so every visit there was still like a pilgrimage. 30 miles had seemed nothing when I had lived 600 miles away with the Minch between us, but sometimes, living there with no car, 30 seemed like 600.

Gravir was almost at the end of a road, (Some people said it was a road to nowhere!) ten miles from the main road (and the nearest hotel bar!) and just another three the other way to the last village, the Minch and a view of Skye and the Shiant isles.

When I finally came to stop there in 1986 I was hit by there being no more 'if onlys'. All my life it had been "If only this, if only that" everything would be better, everything would be alright. Now there were no more if onlys. This was it. It was like coming face to face with myself in a mirror, no holds barred, nothing to hide behind, no-where else to run to; and dealing with that was probably, on one level, what I did for the next ten years. I think I've come out of it a little wiser, a little clearer...

From the very beginning I had intended to home-educate Talie. My three older children went through the school system. My son seemed to suit it and indeed he is now a Primary teacher, but I felt with all of them that once they went to school they weren't really mine any more. I felt more and more guilty that I wasn't educating them myself, but in those days I wasn't living a life where it was possible and I'm not sure that I knew that I could. 'Education Otherwise' has achieved a great deal in the past few decades. I have very clear concepts about the education system and very clear ideas as to why I home educated Talie. These have been re-inforced now that we have returned to England and he has entered school for the first time aged 13. This is as much a clear decision as previously it was to keep him out. I am working now with what we have joined, not confronting it, but it has made me really value what I did those first 8 years. Wherever I'd have lived I'd have home educated during those years, but in Gravir we lived round the corner from the local school and we lived in such a small community. I felt they would think I was an arrogant English woman rejecting their school and I was very apprehensive of telling them. No-one really ever understood why I did it, but it enabled Talie to do everything at his own pace, pursue his own interests fully and through hours and hours and hours of drawing each week, develop his phenomenal artistic talents. It gave us the freedom to be able to go where we wanted when we wanted, but it was another thing that set us apart from people.

I had to learn a lot over the years to understand their attitudes, which were often very different from what I had expected, but in those early days I was still in my somewhat romantic dream, even though I hadn't really gone there to fulfil a dream. I had gone there to bring up my son in a wonderful environment and I had gone there to celebrate and serve the ancient sites, the sacred landscape and the Sleeping Beauty Mountain.

In all this I do not think I have failed, and for a woman living so alone with a young child in that environment, I do not think I could have expected much more of myself.

So now, having set the scene somewhat, as it was in 1986, I want to move on into the great cycle of the year and my celebration of it during that incredible decade I lived on that magical island.

Part Two - The Wheel Of The Year

Chapter 6

Entering The Circle

Talie and I lived over ten years on the Isle of Lewis, from June '86 to late August '96.

I had imagined Lewis would be my base, from where I would continue to venture forth on the same journeys as I had been making before, but that wasn't to be. Just living there took me over almost completely, what with all the summer work; and there was the sense that the Stones, the Mountain and the sacred landscape were saying - "Well you've come here to be with us so why go away?" I felt I had to dedicate myself entirely to that which had brought me there. The occasional trips back to the mainland and to England, sometimes only once every $1\frac{1}{2}$ years, were to sink with some sort of relief into ordinary houses and amble round endless shops, the like of which I had no access to on Lewis. On these trips I rarely wanted to venture out into the landscape of England, unless it was something very specific we wanted to see and usually only when someone took us there. It was only in the latter years that we began once again to make small but powerful journeys on our own into the English landscape; onto the moors of Penwith in Cornwall or round the chalk white horses of Berkshire and Wiltshire. On these trips I was usually also doing business: giving slide and poetry performances and finding outlets where I could sell the cards of my pictures.

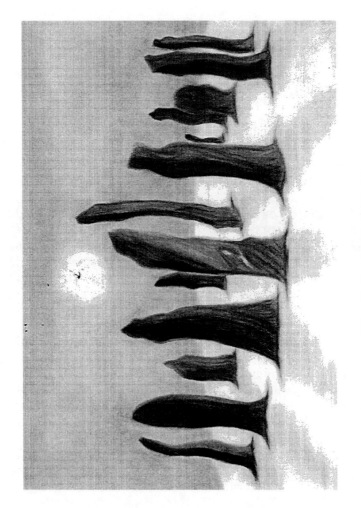

"The Gathering", Callanish

In the early years there were also practical problems. When Talie was a baby I carried him on my front with a rucksack on my back. As he got bigger I put him on my back, but then didn't know how to carry the luggage. For a while I hung bags round my neck, but that was extremely unsatisfactory (and very uncomfortable) and I'm sure I've done some damage to my neck vertebrae. By the time we'd been on Lewis a few months I got him his first buggy and it was back to the rucksack on the back, but everything was much more cumbersome, and when I contemplated lengthy journeys in the Western Isles there was also the problem of where and how to get food when walking only a few miles each day.

Initially I felt a kind of panic that I wasn't doing the great physical journeys through the land any more. I felt that journeying was my 'new' identity and I was afraid of losing it. After a while, though, I realised that I was on a different kind of journey. The circle of the year was the journey, to be repeated over and over by celebrating its festivals at the same places each year; for that is maybe what our ancestors did, returning generation after generation, aeon after aeon to the same sacred sites at the same times of the year and thereby deepening and intensifying that very sacredness and the power and focus of place.

In this way the awareness becomes clear - of time as cyclic, as an ever-turning circle - but perhaps more a spiral than a circle, for it isn't stagnant, just repeating itself, going nowhere; but continually renewing itself, becoming real and fresh, the past constantly part of the present and of the future as well. It is a different state of being. Nowadays we tend to see the past in the past, so that it is no longer part of us, but I believe ancient people perceived the world and reality very differently from how we do now; they didn't see things objectively from a viewpoint somewhere outside and separate from, they just were an integral part of everything. This doesn't make their perception lesser than ours, quite the

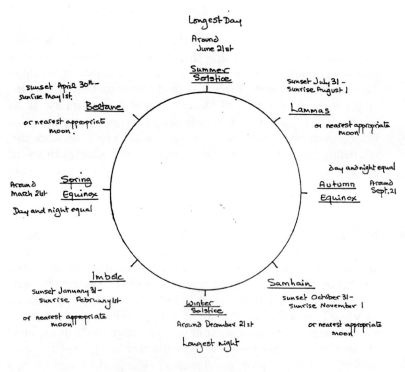

The Cycle of the Year

66

reverse, for I believe this 'knowledge from within' meant they had a far greater understanding of everything and also how everything worked as a whole than we do now.

It seems as though when I journeyed through the whole of Britain I was following the paths of the paleolithic/mesolithic nomadic peoples and when I made this cyclic journey in a physically smaller landscape I followed the paths of the Neolithic more settled farming peoples.

Over the ten years this going again and again to the same places seemed to open up for me the doorways through time, so that time past and people past are easily accessible, just there down a corridor, visible and real, not so much seen from a distance, but as though I could go there and be with them, in a way be them - a kind of direct transmission again. It is very hard to explain in words. It's a state of being.

I tend to be very against most 'whistle-stop' mystical or spiritual tours; the rushing around on a tight itinerary and 'collecting' of ancient sacred sites, crossing them off the tourist list - been there, seen that, taken the photograph, bought the souvenir, and even sometimes, horrendously, planted the crystal. I think sites need time - time to just be with them, in stillness, with no expectation, not imposing anything of one's own on them, but sitting and listening and waiting to see if they have anything to tell. I had to learn that, and that was one of the great teachings of Callanish for me.

In my early days of doing performances at sites I didn't listen enough, although perhaps I did, for I stopped doing it like that and desperately craved solitary time with place. In all the years I spent with Taliesin at sacred sites we did little but sit and be - having with us sacred objects, significant objects, maybe burning candles and incense but taking most of it away except maybe for a flower, a plant, a piece of wood, something that wouldn't disturb the energy of the site, only hopefully enhance it. Somehow we just plugged ourselves in to what was there. It was all very focussed and all very real.

So now I want to turn the cycle of ten years into one. I want to travel round one year and share with you the experiences of ten years, or indeed the experiences of fifteen years, from when I first went there in 1982 - and in fact it isn't finished yet - it goes on, it continues, for I will always be going back. My heart and my spirit still live on Lewis. I'm just physically living away for a while.

Looking back on the years I lived there is like looking on one Great Year. The beginning feels long ago and has its own character; the end feels very recent and is also quite distinct, but all the years in between have merged into one.

Here, then, is the turning of my Great Year on Lewis.

Chapter 7

Winter/Midwinter/
Winter Solstice

I want to enter the circle in the Winter: in the darkest, deepest time of the year. This is a time of pause, where everything seems to stop. I call it the pause in the pendulum's swing. It's like the pause between inhaling and exhaling, where for a moment everything is 'on hold' and everything is potential waiting to be realised. For as long as there is life, that next breath always comes.

I'm sure that it's in our genetic make-up that we slow down in the depth of winter. Although we are not animals that hibernate, there seems some element of hibernation in us. Everything seems to function at a different rate, a changed metabolism. I always feel I am retreating deep into a cave, a safe place in the belly of my mother the earth - and isn't that where many ancient peoples had their sacred places - in deep caves? And where they had no caves, they built them - long barrows and chambered cairns with their womb-tombs indeed formed like the womb of the earth. I feel sure these places which were used to bury but a few of the dead, were the houses of the spirits of the ancestors, the places not only for the physically dead, but the death of shamanic initiation, where the initiates were taken to meet the spirits of those ancestors and the tribal totemic beings. They would be reborn as shaman, priest/ess or wise elder. It is surely likely that this is why these structures were later known as the houses of the sidhe or Faerie Folk by the time the Celts arrived or emerged.

Maybe these ancient people believed in re-incarnation, a cycle of life and death, and those buried there were reborn from the womb of the earth, their mother. In the traditions of some peoples still, parents will go to sacred caves to receive the spirit of a child that will enter an embryo or foetus.

At Samhain, the Celtic New Year, which is at sunset on October 31st, I like to physically enter the earth - "going in for winter"; to physically emerge again at Imbolc three months later, at sunrise on February 1st. I then feel I "am in" wherever I go and whatever I do, for that winter, slowing down and slowing down, going deeper and deeper towards that profound pause of midwinter. It seems crazy to me that the wild extravagance that "Christmas" has become, with all its attendant pace and pressures, goes completely counter to what are our natural instincts, our natural rhythms.

In the winter I feel so close to the Hag, the Cailleach, the spirit of She who watches us through the winter, sees us through - that energy of the life in the seed sleeping in the frozen earth, ready to thrust forth with the coming of spring - the potential of life, the primary cause : the Winter Goddess who holds that potential of life.

It is a time when the ancestors are close, the essence of their wisdom very available to us. It is a time when we almost naturally enter into a state of meditation. As though as the 'busy-ness' of the mind slows down and stills itself, so our minds cease to function in the normal way and we are just in a state of Being. I think many of us feel stress because modern life prevents us doing what is natural, prevents us from this slowing of the natural rhythm. I have heard many women especially say around this time that their brains just don't seem to work properly. I don't think they are meant to.

I think that when we knew how to live, knew how to glean the neccessities of life from our surroundings, we'd have had it all done by then: the food stored and preserved to see us through the winter; the animals that were going to live through, safe in the byre; the fuel stacked outside the door. We just went inside, sat and gazed into the fire and told the tales of the ancestors as we sat knitting or mending the nets. The hurricanes raged outside, but we had everything there close by and unless there was illness or disaster, that was how it was.

Nowadays we fight the rhythms of nature and it is we who suffer.

I believe the ancient great fires of mid-winter were to celebrate the return of the sun, the birth of the new sun, the start of the six months growth to mid-summer. I don't think they thought they had to do it to make the sun come back - they were wiser than that - and if they feasted at mid-winter it was to celebrate the fact that they had got it all in, they had got it all together and they could afford to feast and they gave thanks.

Talie and I used always to go to the main Callanish site for mid-winter night. We never actually camped at mid-winter: I'd maybe hire a van for a couple of days and in the later years we'd sit in our own car.

We'd go and stand to watch the sun set, lighting the sky livid red against black and purple clouds. It always seemed that the stones themselves were the Ancestors, the grandmothers. I certainly feel the spirits and energies of the ancient ones are embedded in the crystal of those stones - and they'd seem to stand and turn and watch that sun-set and I'd stand and watch and be with them in their watching and there we were for that long, long, longest night of the year. We'd then spend the night in the vehicle beside the stones. I'd go out a few times during the night to stand with the stones, with those ancestors, with the sense that stones and people had shared this night for thousands of years - and to be part of that.

When it was dark moon as well, the darkness was total and so deep, so profound.

I never sat all night in the stones at midwinter, because of Talie, but before I lived on Lewis I spent a night in the stones very near to the deep of winter and I felt like a foetus in that womb-tomb, for there is the chamber of a small cairn in the centre of the circle; I felt like a child in the Cauldron of Cerridwen. The ancestor stones seemed to move in close around me and stand so dark and tall and tell me just to get on with it - more or less to pull my finger out - for I had all the knowledge within me. Quite a lesson!

I have been asked why I only refer to 'the Grandmothers' and not to male ancestors. Although there are the spirits of male beings in the stones and there is the presence of male ancestors around, the teachers that I meet there - 'The Old Ones' - are female. Maybe this is because I am a woman and we each find what is there for us, and for me that is 'The Grandmothers', but although I don't believe in an actual matriachy in the distant past, I do believe that thousands of years ago there was a more matrifocal society and maybe it was a company of old women who were the holders of the most esoteric knowledge.

At sunrise we would go once more to sit or stand with the stones. Everything would be vibrant. Having endured that longest night there was the sense of the energy really having turned, that everything really was waxing once more and that somewhere deep in the core of everything there were the first thoughts of growth. There was that sense of relief at having survived something potentially unsurvivable and a deep inner strength because of that. How different it was when winter really was about survival; so unlike the security of modern life for most people. It is good at this time to think how birds and animals still struggle to survive, as do people in less advantaged lands, and that even in this increasingly unfair society there are growing numbers of old people in ill-heated homes and people on the streets who actually won't survive.

So we stood there in this state with everything else that had survived and watched the brilliant gold of the birth of the new sun. The stones, the ancestors, the grandmothers, in the cold light of that dawn, seemed to turn to face the coming of that new sun with us.

We would probably have left a small sprig of mistletoe all night in the chamber in the centre of the stones - the magical tree of the space between years. Usually it was a bit of last year's and a bit of this year's - keeping the continuity going. We usually lit a candle as well; once lit it roared and guttered in the wind, feeding on the wind, hard to blow out. Focussing in on these small things, the reality within us was as vast as the universe. The flame of continuity. Life that goes on. The 'tree' returning, replacing; our life turning - another year gone - another circle engraved, cutting the pattern deeper.

During the long months of winter we were usually alone with the stones at such times as this. In the summer months we would not make these small ritual offerings in the centre of the stones, for it felt too public, too soon to be disturbed by visitors. We would sit by a rocky outcrop to the south of the stones. This was known to Talie and myself as 'Old Grandmother Turtle' and she had a tiny 'cave' between her knees in which we huddled. This unfortunately has been badly disturbed by archaeological excavation in recent years.

With this great peace within us we would return home. I would think of how long those stones had stood there - in hurricane, storm, dark moon, full moon, sunrises, sunsets and the heat of the summer sun and I marvelled at that length of time. 5,000 years. Think of all they have seen! They are like ancient people whose time passes so slowly, and our little lives are such tiny flickers on that time-scale. I would think of them standing, endlessly standing through all those extremes of weather and dark.

We returned to our home and the shopping and our little Christmas festivities. Although the Solstice is the festival in my spiritual calendar, there is a comfort in celebrating at the same time as a lot of other people, especially with a child. Everything finally shuts down and most 'Christmas' things are pagan anyway - the tree, the holly and mistletoe, the Christmas pudding and indeed 'Father Christmas' himself, that old fly agaric eating shaman coming down the smoke-hole; passage between worlds.

In the early days on Lewis I was relieved to be free of the pressures I'd felt being the mother in a family with three children, trying to satisfy the expectations of Christmas, so now I kept it very low key, but as the years passed it became again a difficult time for me. I missed having the choice at least of being with family and it brought home the lonliness that at other times I could keep from myself by the busyness of all I was doing. It was a limbo time when I was looking into that mirror of myself more than at any other time of year. At Christmas and Hogmanay I was not socially part of anything much that was going on around me, and that was painful - at times almost unbearably so.

In the Islands Christmas has only relatively recently been celebrated. I think the Free Church believes it is a pagan festival and they are not into 'celebrating' religious festivals. Hogmanay is the big get-together time. The older people still don't really celebrate Christmas. Their houses aren't decorated and if you visit them they will bring out from somewhere a pile of cards they have received - they are never displayed.

I was glad when all this was over and we could get back to normal. In the early years I was very fearful of the elements.

There is rarely snow at mid-winter - indeed the snowfall is usually fairly slight anyway, it being much warmer than mainland Scotland because of the Gulf Stream drift. What cold there is usually comes in about February. But there is wind. Often terrible wind. I could not at first believe my tin house would stand up to it. People said "Oh, it's stood all these years, it'll stand a few years longer", but I worried not knowing the condition of the wooden structure that supported the metal and feared it would fall like a pack of cards. If the wind had once got in, everything would have gone. I grew to know the wind speed and the wind force on the Beaufort scale by the sounds of the house. 8, which actually is Gale Force was just a wind outside. I was suprised when I realised this was a Gale, for I thought a Gale would be much stronger. Force 9 (Severe Gale) was also a wind outside, but stonger - the sort of wind it's nice to lie in bed listening to as it blows through the trees and you snuggle down because the wind is outside and you are inside. But when it came to Force 10 (Storm Force) it was different. It affected the house; each gust hit the house hard and made it creak. Force 11 (Violent Storm) was horrendous, almost like waves. There would be these silent ominous lulls and then would come another massive 'gust' slamming into the building like something physically attacking it, everything creaking severely.

Nothing rattled, because if it was that loose it would have blown off long ago. Force 12 (Hurricane) was unbelievable and I lived through quite a few during those years on Lewis. They usually happened at night and in the dark they sounded even worse, but once there was one in daylight: the wind vibrated along the corrugated walls because it was coming from the West, not the South-West and I stood watching from the window. The trees outside were horizontal and I watched amazed as birds hopped along the ground into the wind. If they'd have gone with the wind, of course, they would have been smashed to bits. Is that what "Flying in the face of the wind" means? I was just amazed they were out in it at all. I thought they would have hidden away somewhere. I gained great respect for my house on that occasion, for it remained intact with only the gatepost blowing out and the dustbin going down the road.

One New Year I was out at a neighbour's and there was an incredible wind. I returned apprehensively and was most relieved to find the house still standing. I went to bed. In the morning I saw all sorts of bits of wood all over the place outside, torn from the roof at strange angles. 3 hours later I thought I'd better check right round the building, only to find the door of the hall had blown in and the end wall had blown out at the bottom. There was a gap of over a foot. It looked like a depressurised aircraft. Everything from the room was jammed into the gap as though it had been sucked out. Miraculously, the huge window had remained intact in the sloping wall. The advantage of the wood and metal house was that it could be sledge-hammered back into place and as soon as the builders merchants opened after Hogmanay, it only took the joiner a day to repair it, working a lot of the time by oil-light. That was more than a hurricane, I think. It must have been more like a tornado and of course, with global warming, these are now becoming increasingly common in England and Wales.

Although you can't actually go out in weather like that, if you are out in the wind it's a lot safer than in England. In the Hebrides such weather is normal and everything loose or potentially so is weighted down, tied down, chained down, cemented in...In England winds still tend to come as a surprise and all sorts of potentially life-threatening things fly around, and of course, people do die.

It's incredible when such a wind is over. You feel like a limp rag as you watch the wintry sun struggle through and realise you are still here, you have survived. It used to be weird sometimes sitting by the fire listening to the radio with this almost unnatural normalness going on indoors, this strange stillness... yet outside there's this incredible raging - and if, in a moment, that raging was to burst inside.......

After the wind I'd once again feel at one with those birds that also had survived - one more time - and the trees still standing and the poor sheep out in it all. The sheep tended to survive the winter and then die exhausted in the spring. Of course, when the wind passed and everything went still, it was probably only the eye of the storm, and there was the whole other arm of the spiral of the wind yet to come; it was a bit like when I got to Australia and realised I'd got to fly all the way back again!

The last winter that we lived there was cold. I feel this was not unconnected to the destruction of a unique and ancient cairn to the north of the Callanish main circle, which was bulldozed away for the purposes of road widening on the day before the Winter Solstice that year.

I actually loved this last extreme cold spell in the winter of 1995/6. We settled down for Christmas: our stack of peats outside, plenty of Calor Gas, paraffin, candles, radio batteries and food and were merrily celebrating. We were listening to Radio One and a news bulletin informed us that many power cables were down in the Western Isles and everyone was without electricity. We laughed a bit. They were without it quite a long while. Many cables are accessible only by helicopter, including one not far from the back of our house! I've rarely seen such thick snow on Lewis as that year - deep blue-black skies lowering over a white world. When the sun came out, the skies and all the shadows were a rich blue. It was amazing.

We got through without a frozen pipe although it was 10 degrees below zero in parts of the house. I left the only tap running and kept getting up in the night to flush the toilet.

Sometimes it only just made it. It was only when it suddenly thawed and a main further up the road burst that we were without water. We wore loads of clothes and hats indoors - even in bed. People used to live like that always. The windows were thickly encrusted with Jack Frost's handiwork and except in the main room that had the fire, these never melted until the big thaw came, but I didn't feel all that cold. It wasn't windy and all the moisture in the air was frozen onto the windows. It was really dry and still and I began to understand how people can live in places like Siberia or Alaska. Once it got warmer and the air was damp, I felt cold - that cold that gets into your bones.

We were better off than many of the modern homes - such as the council houses which had open fires with back boilers. When their pipes froze they couldn't light the fire, or the boiler would explode. However, people up there take it all in their stride, though they might moan a bit.

I'm glad I had that real winter before I left the Island.

Chapter 8

Imbolc (1st February) Brighde's Day

One of the joys of being as far north as the Outer Isles is that although the depth of winter is so dark and long, once the light starts to come back it happens fast and you really notice it. Even by New Year it has noticeably shifted, and there is a date - I think it is January 17 - which, I was told by the old lady at the Post Office, is the day when "we have an extra hour of light". By the time Imbolc comes, there is a lot more light. It's all relative, isn't it, compared with what has gone before. It made me even more intensely aware of the energy of Imbolc - Brighde's Day.

The Celts began their celebrations at sunset on the eve of a day, as they celebrated their new year on the eve of the dark of the year, so Imbolc begins at sunset on January 31st. Brighde was such an important being to the peoples of Britain and Ireland that when Christianity came here they had to turn her into St.Bridget and incorporate other legends into hers. Christianity celebrates Candlemas on February 2nd and this really is the same thing.

Brighde is, in a way, the spirit of the Outer Isles. Maybe she was the ancient Goddess of the land. She is a very real presence, a very real energy, there still. I feel that over the years I lived there, I came to truly know her as a very real being. When Christianity came to the Islands she was very easily turned into St.Bridget. She was most beloved by the island people who called on her through prayers and

"Brighde of the Isles", Melbost, Borve, Isle of Lewis

incantations for help in many activities throughout the day. She was called on as aid-woman for women giving birth and for a great deal of healing. There is much to be found about her in the 'Carmina Gaedelica' by Alexander Carmichael. He went around gathering these prayers etc. from people who had lived before the Free Church came to the Islands. After that it was all put down as superstition.

Brighde seems to have a very strong 'personality' - serene, mature, self-contained and very strong - one to turn to for strength, to hold onto in crisis. Often I seem to have felt her hand on my shoulder or sensed her standing just behind and to one side of me, and have felt that strength flow into me.

I do not think of Brighde in a diminutive way. Although Imbolc may be the death of Winter, the end of the reign of the Hag aspect and the birth of the new and young, she is not a child. The renewal is a renewal of her strength. She is always there, but at her time of year her strength is very powerfully apparent.

So now we are past that depth of winter and are looking forward with our own strength that grows with the light, to the coming year and all that has to be done. She personifies that.

The second winter we were on Lewis we celebrated Imbolc rather like the people used to. The women used to make a Brighde doll from a sheaf of oats, dress and decorate her and make a bed of rushes for her. They would feast and invite the men in later! They would stand at the door and call to Brighde that her bed was ready and entreat her to enter their house. They would lay a willow wand in the bed. They would smooth the ashes of the fire. In the morning they would look for Brighde's footprint in the ashes and if it was there know she had been and their household was blessed for the coming year. I have rarely known anything I have done in a house that was so powerful. We called her in, and I know she came and I feel she has been with me ever since - wherever I go. There were many more traditions celebrating her and incantations about 'the Serpent coming from the Mound' which seem to be about the awakening of the life force and energy in the land.

Imbolc was one of the major events of our calendar. Occasionally we went to sit at dawn beside a waterfall that fell vertically by the side of Gravir's loch, Loch Odhairn, but whatever else we did, we always went to a well dedicated to Brighde in the North West of Lewis at a place called Melbost, Borve. I believe there are three wells dedicated to saints in this village, which seems unusual in this land of the Free Church. Bride's Well (Tobar Brighde) is a small, humble place in a field which is part of a croft. It has a sort of little dolmen over it, though the capstone is covered with cement. A local man always used to come over to tell me "It was only built in the 20's you know", but I wondered if it was just the covering that was constructed then. It seems to be a natural spring, flowing down to the sea. Its water is clear and pure and beautiful.

Nearby is the ruin of an oval building and many stones that are like megaliths. The building seems to be made from the huge pebbles rolled by the sea onto the shore. This also is dedicated to Brighde, a Brighde chapel. It is an incredible place and it is the place to celebrate Brighde. She always seems to be there and most particularly to come to you at that time. In the cement on the capstone of the well is the imprint of a single horseshoe. I don't think this is the hoofprint of a passing pony, somehow; it is very deliberately placed there, seemingly symbolic of 'Brighde of smithcraft'.

In the early years that we visited, it seemed well-tended and was surrounded by a wire fence with a gate to keep the sheep out. I used to think there must be a little old Cailleach who looked after it. In recent years, however, it has seemed more neglected; indeed when we returned in April 1997, not having been able to get back to Lewis for Imbolc that year, the grass was growing in thick mats over the little stream flowing from it and it almost seemed blocked. The fence gradually fell down and the gate rotted and broke. I feel I need always to go there at least once a year to make sure it's alright. (I've since contacted local people there, and I'm hoping it will be fenced off again and looked after.)

We would go there on Imbolc Eve and see the sun set over the sea. We would usually spend the night sleeping near the sea in a hired van or in our own car. If we couldn't make it for the night we would drive there for the dawn - Sun rise on Brighde's Day. Beautiful. If we were there for the night I would go out to sit a while in the dark by the well. We always drank some of her water and brought some away with us, and we would give her a gift of some from the previous year - those returning cycles again. If we had been away to England I would bring her a gift also of some water from Chalice Well in Glastonbury and then I would take water from Brighde's well as a gift when I went to Glastonbury. These exchanges, these links, feel important.

We used to sit by the well with all sorts of little goddess figurines. I had a little statuette my older children had given me one year for Mother's Day. I call it my 'Smith Goddess' for she holds a hammer and stands by an anvil. I have one figure which is a piece of driftwood. Always, after being with the well, we would go to a part of the shore where driftwood would be washed up in the winter storms. I always found lots, many goddess-shaped and all somehow like small versions of the Callanish Stones, which are themselves like the figures of the ancestors, the grandmothers. I always found this truly remarkable. This 'Brighde shore' (my name for it) is such a special place although it doesn't really look all that amazing. The Atlantic waves roll and crash onto the rocks and shore -

even when it is a still full-moon night. Often you can feel the earth vibrate with the thundering of the waves.

The first year I ever went there, in 1983, before I had Talie, was an epic journey. I had hitched up from Suffolk and had all sorts of adventures on the way, then camped behind a wall in what was virtually a kiddies garden tent. A violent storm blew up with incredible winds and hailstones. The tent completely collapsed into a mere bag. However, it was full moon and the skies were mostly clear and I struggled out several times during the night to sit by the well and lie in the oval ruin lashed by the icy wind, taken into another reality and given teachings I somehow had to unravel over the subsequent years. In these later years with Talie, we would sit a while before leaving, watching the Oystercatchers - known to the Gaels as Brighde's bird - the Ghillie-Brighde - Brighde's servant. I never was able to grow snowdrops up there but feel sure in my heart that this is Brighde's flower and that the willow is her tree.

From Melbost, Borve we would drive down to Callanish. It would still feel quite early in the morning. I would emerge from the cairn in the centre of the stones feeling that now I had come out from the winter, out from the cave, out from the womb of the earth. Reborn. Always so wonderful to share these times with the stones. Sometimes they seemed so vibrant, so alive. Sometimes in the middle of the day, especially in the summer with lots of tourists around, they seemed to withdraw themselves, seeming smaller, just like ordinary stones...but at these times....

Then we'd go home, burn some of the less goddess-like driftwood on the fire, it spitting with the salt from the sea, and when we could, eat oatcakes and Ewe's milk cheese. If we could bake our own bannock we would. And share it with Brighde.

If Imbolc/Oimelc means Ewe's Milk, I wonder if that was an Irish name, for there were only a few lambs on Lewis at that time of year. Most didn't come until April or May. I'd find it strange if I went to England in March and the lambs were already large and oldish, yet get back to Lewis and they weren't even born. Of course, once upon a time England was a Celtic land. People tend to forget that.

One vivid memory I have of Brighde's time, was that it was when we might experience the Aurora Borealis (Northern Lights). I didn't see them that many times in 10 years, mainly because our house faced South and we backed onto a hill to the North, so I'd only see this extraordinary phenomenon if I was out anyway or if I felt it was the kind of night when they might manifest and I just kept watching. They would come on a clear night, be seen best at dark moon, and the first clue of their imminence would be a kind of white rainbow across the sky and then great searchlights or wafting veils would rise up and move and pulsate across the heavens. I found it totally unlike anything else of life on earth. I used to feel I was in another realm, another reality. It was like that veil between the worlds. Things like this I miss very much. When they came at Imbolc, which they sometimes did, it was the most powerful and overwhelming gift from Brighde herself; an affirmation somehow that somewhere, on some level, one was doing something right.

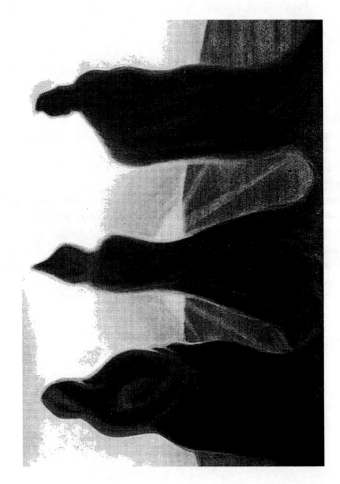

"Mother, Maiden and Crone", Equinox sunrise, Callanish

Chapter 9

Spring Equinox and the Coming of Spring

Sometimes the worst weather came after Imbolc: the snow if there was any, the nights of deep frost, but the days were growing longer and lighter and it didn't seem so bad. Even though a night may be freezing the sun of the day was higher and hotter and often the ice would melt. It was easier to cope with. Whereas if it froze at midwinter there was no power in the sun and it seemed it never would thaw.

The Western Isles Council (Comhairle nan Eilean) is excellent at keeping most of its few roads clear. Mountains of salt get spread around the islands into small piles by roadsides and many a winter morning is heralded by the flashing yellow lights of "the gritter". You get so used to things. I was amused in recent years, driving with a visitor to the islands past a strange white and brown mound, when she asked excitedly "What's that?" only to be told it was the salt for the roads! The sheep love it. They have no salt licks and just stand in the middle of the roads licking the salt all winter. They think they own the roads up there anyway. Quite often I've been held up by a ewe standing in the middle of the road suckling her lamb, oblivious to traffic. When you walk past sheep, they run away, but fast cars have no effect on them at all (except actually killing them quite often because of this). They sit on the roads at night because the black tarmac surface is warmer than the frozen earth. A long line of their eyes in the headlights looks like faerie lanterns illuminating the roadsides as they eerily watch us mortals.

As it approached the spring Equinox (around March 21st give or take a day or two's variation either side per year), I would just revel in the amount of light after so long in the dark. Suddenly there seemed time for things. In the dark of winter there seemed only time, once it was light, to get washed and dressed, do all the chores, get the fuel in for that night, fill the lamps, make sure all the candles were renewed, do all the washing (by hand) and generally get sorted, before it began to get dark again. If there was time for anything else, it would only be for one thing and if I were to cook a proper meal, then that would be the one thing. If I wanted to do anything else, I wouldn't get a meal cooked. In the evenings, in the dark, I couldn't do much that was creative - could sometimes write letters, do accounts, type things up by candlelight, but not much else. We would have lovely times though, cooking pancakes on the open fire, making candles in yogurt pots from all the old candle-ends, and a lot of reading aloud to Talie, even when he was quite old. It was our substitute for the telly - and much more enjoyable. Quite honestly, as each midwinter turned I don't think I actually believed the days would grow longer again and it always seemed like a miracle when they did.

So - oh, what joy when the days did grow and there was time to do several things after the chores. I began to relax and realised how stressful the dark and the winter had been, having to work so hard and so frantically to get everything done in that window of daylight. When the days were dull in the winter, even daytime things became impossible. You can't sweep the carpet and clean if it's too dark to see the dirt! That wonderful sense of unwinding was such an enormous relief.

Actually I found that mid-point between summer and winter solstices, between extremes, in some ways the most comfortable time of the year. Midsummer would almost bring a different kind of stress. Midsummer was a crazy time. You could work all night and then when did you sleep? But when half the time was light and half dark, it felt well-balanced. A bit of dark evening felt nice: a reward after a busy day. In the summer you just never stopped.

We used always to go to Callanish for the Spring Equinox. Some people say Callanish is a lunar, not a solar site, but I don't believe the Neolithic people created these structures for just one purpose. They were multi-functional, multi-pupose, and the functions were all inter-twined. In some ways, part of their science; in other ways, part of their spirituality, their deep and ancient mythology, for it was for them all one. It wasn't all separated and compartmentalised as it is in our world now. It was all part of that one thing - life. Even death was part of life. Art wasn't "Art", music wasn't "Music", astronomy wasn't "Astronomy", it was all part of life, and these great stone circles weren't there just for one reason. People would ask me "What's your theory about the stones?" and I'd say "I don't have a theory". I think everyone's theory is probably part of the truth to a greater or lesser extent, but no one theory is the complete and perfect explanation. Vision needs opening out much more widely. Their experience of the universe on many levels was very different from ours, and it is ours that has narrowed down - drastically.

I do think Callanish was a lunar site. It was a lot to do with the moon, with the dark, with night, with winter, with aspects of death, but not in a negative way. Maybe the full rich experience of night, dark and winter is something we have lost from our lives. Whatever the purpose and function of the stones themselves and as part of a sacred landscape, that world and life and people that functioned with them has gone and we are with them now, and if their presence and their form fulfills for us a function that nothing else in our life does, then that is part of their role now. For me, now, this site is also solar.

In the early days of living there, this would be our first hitch of the year and usually our first camp, even though there often would be the snow that was absent at midwinter - and sometimes horizontal hail. Sometimes it was a hard camp (for me, Talie never seemed bothered). We'd line the tent with newspaper and cardboard, but it was a tiny tent and ever so cosy. After a few years I did get a bit weary, though, of crawling in and out with boggy knees and the endless struggle to put on and take off my wellies, but there you go, the price you pay.

When Talie was young I could never find the right clothes for him; the right waterproofs and things you could easily undo to change nappies. They don't seem to make the proper clothes for little children to go camping in the Hebrides, or even to be pushed around in a buggy in the rain, I don't know why. Even now when he's 13, I find it difficult to get waterproof trousers his size without resorting to ski-wear that costs far more than I can afford.

It was so good to get on the road again with the pack on my back. I'd feel I was me again, back in the real and vibrant world. There was something almost unreal about winter and I never felt quite like me - not this nomadic me anyway. The nomad spirit would leap for joy and just ache to get on the road as spring came. Living claustrophobically inside the house all winter was like living inside my own head, my own skull; everything going round and round and getting nowhere.

We'd always stop on the way to Callanish at the same gorse bush, for on the Celtic Tree Calendar Gorse is the tree of the Spring Equinox. We'd ask the bush if we could pick a few sprigs (not easy with gorse). I always ask trees and plants if I can pick them and somehow seem to know whether or not I have permission. Sometimes it is no. I never take much and it always has to be for a purpose. Here it was to mark another station on the turning of the year. I'd always have a piece from the previous year with me, and sometimes from other equinoxes in other places. It's all part of that cycle, that turning, returning, continuity....

Callanish main circle (there are quite a few other circles nearby in this incredible neolithic landscape) is laid out like a Celtic cross. There is the circle of 13 stones and in the centre one great tall stone and the remains of the cairn. To East, South and West there are stone rows like 'arms' and to the North a great long avenue. From above it looks like a dancing figure. The arms to east and west are almost truly aligned, so for me it is very much an Equinox place. To see on the two equinoctial days of the year when the sun really does rise in the east and set in the west, it actually do that beyond the ends of these arms, is as though one watches a megalithic dancer catch the sun in the morning, throw it, like a juggler, across the sky and catch it in the other hand at sunset. It also feels as though the energy of the sun rolls along one arm, spirals around in the centre of the circle and rolls away along the other arm to the sun set. When you bear in mind there was a cairn in that centre, with its entrance to the east, there is much food for thought as to how that solar energy functioned in the cycle of death and rebirth. Of course there must also have been times when rising full moons would have shone on that entrance.

At that unique site I was so aware of the balance of the equinox day - half light, half dark; east to west; the point, the fulcrum between the solstices, and yet it isn't a time of balanced energy. After the pause and stillness of midwinter and the coming pause at the height of midsummer, the equinoxes seem to rush past so fast - a very speedy time, often a wild time.

It was good to be there for a few days, to slow the pace down, to be there for sunset, sunrise and sunset again - the full circle. I was very aware of the Circle; aware of the semi-circle of the sun in our sky going down beneath the horizon to be the semi-circle of day on the other side of the earth. All about circles. Often there was also the semi-circle of a rainbow. The wild time was often a time of dynamic and changeable weather - a very rainbow time. The skies would go a deep dark blue-black, yet a narrow band of clear sky above the horizon would allow the sun to shine on the stones lighting them a brilliant white or gold, and then the rainbows, double or even treble, would come.

One thing about Lewis that many people say, is that it is the place where the earth meets the sky. It is so true.

Over the years I met many 'beings' in the stones. They were like people, these individual ancestors, some maybe personifications or manifestations of ancient gods and goddesses, ancient spirits of the land; some the spirits of shamanic animals and beings. One stone, near the East of the circle, showed herself to me one Spring Equinox as a 'goddess' - Eostara. She seemed to be a combination of Eostre, the goddess of spring, and Green Tara. She was indeed the green time of the year, taking the wand from Brighde as the circle of the year turned.

There were always just two daffodils that had managed to bloom in our garden in the shelter of the trees in time for the Equinox and we brought them for Eostara. We would leave these with the gorse in the centre of the circle for the night and then at sunrise burn a yellow candle beside them and then place them at Eostara's feet and leave them there. I felt truly blessed the first time I met her.

I used to stand in the circle and feel I was at the centre of every turning circle: atoms, stones, sun, moon, stars, earth, solar system, galaxy, universe and every cycle that turns on every possible level of reality. Circles within circles within circles......

While we camped at Callanish we would go on long walks, which became almost like ritual journeys, and we'd visit some of the people of Callanish. There was Annie Macleod, and her sister Ishbel who taught me how to put ladders on roofs single-handed (they were thick wood and very heavy and awkward) and much else, like how to make it easy to pick up full sacks of peat and how to keep the bags open when you were filling them in the wind; and Mary who'd taken us in for the weekend in 1985. We could never visit more than one person a day, for it is Island hospitality to give you platesful of sandwiches, cake and biscuits with a cup of tea, and you have to eat it all!

Chapter 10

Salmon

When my first springtime on Lewis came, I noticed something rather strange: helicopters flying back and forth over our house with things like dustbins swinging about underneath them. I made enquiries and discovered they were moving the young salmon smolts from the hatcheries to the sea-lochs and it was quicker (and safer for the fish!) to do it by air than to take them round the coast by sea.

I had noticed the square cages in many of the lochs and thought how ugly they looked, but over the months I became more aware of the industry of Fish Farming. It was hailed as the great new scheme for jobs and money for the islands. At first there were lots of little businesses, some run by local communities or individuals, but most of them eventually got bought up by the multi-nationals. It affected me deeply. On the environmental level there was a lot of pollution from the salmon feed, the dye (Canthaxanthin) used to colour the flesh of the salmon (deprived of the diet they had in the wild, their flesh was grey!), and the organophosphates and other substances used to kill the lice on the fish. It was initially done in a very lax way, though after a lot of criticism the industry did tidy itself up quite a lot, but what affected me more than anything was the plight of the fish.

They call the salmon the 'King of the Sea' (and I suppose you could say Queen of the Sea as well) and their life cycle is fantastic. They go from fresh water to salt, travel vast distances through the oceans of the world, then return to the river they first came from, leaping upstream against all the odds to spawn at the place where they were hatched. To deny a creature like that its freedom, deny all its natural instincts, trap it where it can be mauled by passing seals with no chance of getting away is to me the utmost cruelty. They were supposed to surround the cages with predator nets, but frequently didn't. It's like caging an eagle. I know all the arguments they come up with, but I also have mine.

I became very aware of the spirit of Salmon, the wise salmon of ancient myth, the oldest being from the oldest age in some stories, and of the spirit of the wild salmon - still free, but for how long? I knew people who campaigned on other environmental issues who felt it didn't matter if the wild fish died out, for there were plenty in the cages, but it doesn't work when you release these into the wild; their homing patterns don't work properly.

Annie Macleod used to tell us how, when she was young, living by East Loch Roag on the opposite shore from Callanish, she would go to her back door of an evening and the loch was silver with the salmon. There just aren't that many any more. One year Talie and I camped one night at this place - Linshader. We sat there on a still and sunny afternoon and evening when it hadn't rained for weeks. The salmon were waiting for the spate and they leaped and danced for us for hours and hours. All that pent up energy. I had never seen anything like it.

The next day we crossed an old bridge over the river which the salmon were waiting to go up. It was almost dry, yet still a few were desperately slithering over the rocks and up the trickle, so great was that need, that urge, that drive to get to the spawning ground. Mostly they die after that great journey and the spawning. A few survive, mostly female, despised by fishermen; they are known as Kelts. They are like old cailleachs, cocking a snoot at nature, tough as old boots - the Salmon version of the Hag. Sometimes I identified with them, refusing to give up, raising my fist to the universe when it dealt me yet another bad hand. These are my heroines.

There seems to be a relationship between the Salmon and the Callanish stones themselves. The Lewisian Gneiss with its wood-like grain and incredible folds actually looks like salmon flesh. Much of the stone is salmon pink, especially at sunrise or sunset. There is a stone in the avenue of the main circle that seems to me to have a creature in it which is Salmon - the Salmon Spirit - the ancient totemic being. In 1983, there for the summer solstice, I had sat in the stones on the full moon night with Lynne Wood, and the salmon were in the loch below and a lot of naughty poachers (indeed it seemed half the village) were down at the water, and I remember the sight of a man coming up over the hill and through the circle carrying salmon, dripping silver from his hands, and it seemed it was the very moonlight that was dripping - from moon to sea to salmon to stone circle.

In a place like the Hebrides I admit to having an ambivalence about the killing of animals for food. There, human and animal are still part of a cycle. When someone keeps a sheep, then kills and eats it, at least they know what they are doing and it isn't like this stuff in plastic in supermarkets which people pretend was never the body of a live animal. However, it shocked me when I learned that the salmon from the cages were killed when they were 'harvested'. I thought if you took them out of the water they died, but it seems that they have to be bashed on the head by something large and heavy.

The salmon from the fish farms aren't even to provide food for the people of the island - they are for the affluent of south east England. There the fish soon became so common that it was one of the cheapest on the slab. Salmon and chips at the Chippie, really cheap. When the label says "Scottish Salmon" it doesn't mean a wild beast that leapt the rivers of the Highlands, it means it was out of a cage.....

It is difficult when there is so little work in a place like this. You want people to stay there, making a living in a real way without it becoming a tourist theme park or like shortbread tins, but there's still right and wrong ways of doing it. In passing, it occurs to me I don't want to use descriptions like 'remote'. Remote from what? When you live there, you're there, it's not remote. It's London, or even Glasgow that's remote. Mind you, up Callanish way, people refer to South Lochs as 'the back of beyond'.

I digress....

I didn't want to knock the Fish Farming to begin with, but after a while I found out so much that shocked me that I began writing about it. An article, edited without my approval, was published in 'Resurgence'. When someone in the Islands read it, all hell was let loose. I was thenceforward stereotyped as the typical Englishwoman with all her attendant lack of credibility. I cared about the feelings of a fish!!! It just confirmed all their prejudices.

Sometimes, though, there are just things you have to do if you follow your heart. Why should I not criticise something I felt strongly about? Why, because I was an incomer, a stranger to their culture and their ways, should I not criticise something when I felt it to be wrong?

There is no farming of the land any more, just this artificial rearing of artificial fish. There are farmed mussels as well, but that seems a more natural process, somehow. I think the mussels just cling to ropes hanging under rafts.

Chapter 11

Spring

I missed the Springtimes of England. The light was growing, but with no trees and nothing much else springlike happening, there was an energy of Spring that I missed. The daffodills came eventually, and the lambs, many of them born by the roadside, but by then it was almost summer.

When it came to mid-April, I'd be thinking about the peats. I would probably already have had the ladder on the roof if it had been fine and made a start to painting it with expensive red oxide. I aimed to do between a quarter and a third of the roof each year, patching the rusty bits with bitumen and banging in any loose nails. I liked sitting on the roof gazing out over everything. Believe it or not, I suffer from vertigo, and to begin with it was quite hard for me, but it was incredible over the years how at home I became up there, crawling all over the place away from the ladder and inching along the ridge. I aimed to do some of the wall most years as well - in grey oxide. There were also a lot of repairs to do to the window frames, and they needed re-painting. There was an awful lot of roof, an awful lot of wall and an awful lot of window-frames!

It took me all summer to do the peats. The crofters had specially allocated banks - straight, level and well-drained, but I had to find old banks that had been abandoned and not cut for years. Some were only one cut deep, instead of two or three, and they were all up and down and all over the place. It was a wonderful experience though; the gift of the earth.

Working along the length of the bank and something over a foot in from the edge, you start by 'turfing' - that is slicing off the top layer of earth, grass, moss and heather. (There are also many wild plants, including the carniverous sundews. Some years, the lichen blooms.) You put this down on a bare bit of ground where last year's peat was cut, so the plants keep on growing and the surface is just moved down a metre or so. The peat grows back, too, after hundreds of years. They won't allow it to be cut commercially, and the whole centre of the island is uninhabited, so it isn't going to run out. Fewer people now cut peat each year, anyway. The ancient people lived in the centre of the island, I believe, before there was peat, as well as on the coast, so there's an awful lot of history buried under a great depth of peat. Three thousand years ago the climate was different - warm and dry, then the weather changed and the wet came, and with it the peat. Before this the Neolithic people had farmed, indeed the land under the Callanish stones had been cultivated. The peat had grown five feet up the Stones before it was cleared 150 years ago, so only the tops had been sticking out of the ground for a long time until then.

The peat is so acid, of course, and stones in it are bleached white. My banks had already had a complete layer of at least a metre deep cut from them, so I was cutting the bottom metre or more - down literally to "rock bottom". This meant I must have been cutting stuff three thousand years old at the very base. More of this later. The "black" peat is the best. Like black butter when it's cut, it dries to a quarter of it's original size and burns hot - almost one step from coal. The 'brown' is more fibrous, but with interesting textures, shrinks less, but can be harder to dry. Oh, dear, I'm coming over terribly nostalgic!

So this was the beginning of the work. It took me a long time to learn a lot of the tricks, like laying them to dry on ground that wasn't wet for a start! Of course I didn't grow up learning how to do it and never did it as well as if I'd been born to it, but I think I did incredibly well for a Londoner. It felt so familiar, as though I had been doing it for lifetimes, rather like when I held my first baby or tied the bottom of my first basket....so who knows.....I had one strange deja vu type 'memory'. I kept thinking with a panic that I had dropped and lost my wedding ring in the peat. I don't wear a wedding or any other kind of ring...

The first year I cut peats with a spade, but the second year I had a proper peat iron made. The blacksmith makes the iron, then you take it to the joiner and he makes the wooden handle and the part that the iron fits onto, then you take that back to the blacksmith to have it hammered on hard. Some people leave the whole thing soaking in water all winter so that the wood stays swelled and the iron stays on - as you would to keep iron tyres on wooden cart wheels - but mine was so well hammered on it didn't need that.

Chapter 12

Beltane - 1st May

And then it was Beltane. In England Beltane is Spring, but
up there it is so very nearly summer. It's getting so light; a
couple of weeks later it won't get properly dark at all. May
and June are the summer up there. It's the light that makes
the summer.

We would pick a bit of hawthorn from a tree by the old school
in Gravir. The leaves were only just coming: tiny green buds.
We'd go at dawn on Beltane eve - dawn that was already so
early - and then we'd go to Callanish. The land would be dry
now, heather crunching underfoot. We had such a special
place we used to camp. We could look out over the whole of
Callanish and the Sleeping Beauty Mountain. We'd collect
driftwood and have an open fire. It was an old sheep fank, an
old bothy, a walled enclosure - I heard many more romantic
explanations, but who knows? My friends had used it in
'80,'81 and years after; now it felt we were guarding it and
keeping something going. For a long time hardly any one else
camped there, but over the later years, as we went in a car
and camped less, other people used it more and its character
and energy changed, and walls were pulled down. It never
really recovered from the 'Harmonic Convergence' when a
group of people pulled it to bits on many levels. It now feels
like something from our past, something that has gone.

We'd lie there at night and listen to the haunting sound of the
snipe. The first time in the year we camped when the snipe
were there they would dive-bomb us, as though we were
intruding on their space, or maybe they were just curious, for

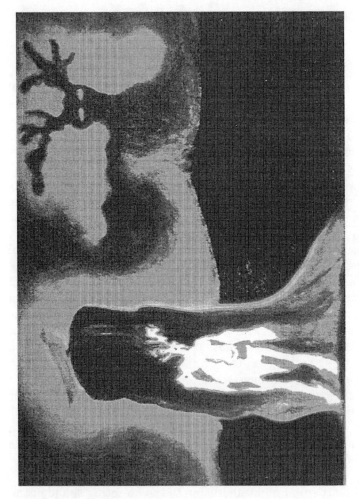

"Beltane at Callanish"

they didn't keep it up. There was one time a bird stood on our tent, but I suppose that's nothing - they stand on the backs of sheep.

There are many legends associated with Callanish, especially at the time of Beltane. All the fires were extinguished in the village and the new fire lit and shared among everyone, as in many places. You were supposed to enter the stones from the South at Beltane. I thought that sounded rather Christian - like the North door of a church being the Devil's, but since the remains of the unique cairn were discovered in direct line from the northern avenue, I feel maybe that avenue was a spirit path, a death road, a passage for the spirits between that cairn and the one in the centre of the stones.

It is supposed to be very auspicious if you hear your first cuckoo in the Callanish stones at Beltane. The story goes that all the cuckoos go for the winter to Tir nan Og (the Otherworld 'land of youth') and fly back from there in the Spring and come and circle round Callanish before flying off to wherever they are going. The reason they don't nest is because if they did they would be tied to the earth and never able to return to Tir nan Og. The first year we lived on Lewis we sat at Callanish for the Beltane dawn and sure enough, there came the cuckoo flying around the stones and then off to wherever. It was our first cuckoo of the year and it felt a very good omen. It never happened to us again.

I had never seen a cuckoo until I went to Lewis. In England one hears them, but they are hidden in trees. Up there, there are no trees, and I saw this strange long bird sitting on a telephone wire, and then it 'cuckoo'd' and I realised what it was.

We were always so alone. I had expected that that far into the year there would be others, but it was always just us. It was very wonderful to be there on our own, getting so profoundly involved with the stones, and I am so grateful for all that time I had throughout the winter, just to be alone with them; but at Beltane, the energy of the time seemed to mock my lonliness. I felt that, at this time of union, this coming together of the powerful forces of the male and female in nature, I should not be so very alone. I was alone with my son, but I was alone.

There is an amazing figure on one of the stones. To me it is the form of Cernunnos, the horned god. He stands with a strange horned headdress and is very well-endowed. He faces the sunset at the Beltane time of year and is lit a deep orange as that red setting orb shines on him. We'd often see extraordinary cloud formations at this time, great beings in the fiery sky echoing the forms in the stones.

There is another stone which I met in later years in the depth of the dark one Beltane night and she was a powerful motherly energy, seeming to reach out her hand to touch my head and comfort me. She is my Beltane Lady. She has another small figure sitting at her feet which catches the light of the rising sun. It looks like a May Queen.

When we sat there alone we always felt so connected with other groups of people and their Beltane fires all over the land, part of some great celebration. I always felt very connected to other places and people when I was at Callanish, indeed on the island as a whole, as though all the channels were very open, the lines of communication very clear. In England things seem much more cluttered, fogged up and cut off. Depends where you sit and what you do, I suppose.

After the Beltane sunrise we'd go back and sit by our camp fire and have a cup of tea. That was our Beltane fire - and it was still so early. I had felt from long years back that it is so special to be up and out with the dawn. Then you are really part of the day and the day belongs to you.

One year I noticed that every house had a white flag flying at the gatepost. I asked what it was and was told there would be a wedding. People fly the white flags on the route the couple will travel. I presume it is a blessing on the wedding. I've never heard of that anywhere else. A Beltane wedding. At Callanish.

There was another energy that manifested at Beltane: the energy of the wild mare, maybe of the wild horse goddesses of the Celts, such as Epona or Rhiannon. (Well, Epona was Roman, but I think in England she just took over the identity of the horse goddess already here).

One year the energy of the Wild Mare had really entered and built up in our lives. Talie had become totally involved in the chalk white horses of South Britain and spent months doing little else but draw and study them. We were about to go down to do a walk, a pilgrimage, round these white horses, honouring the spirit of the Wild Mare which continued right through from the ancientness of Uffington to the stiff figures cut one or two hundred years ago.

For Beltane, we went to Bosta beach, on the island of Great Bernera and there seemed to be something there which rolled in with the 'white horses' of the wild waves; something which really was the energy of that wild horse goddess. It affected Talie very deeply. Later we went to Callanish and sat in the car saying - "Well, at least there's not a horse in the stones", only to look up at one tall stone at the end of the avenue and see that there was indeed the figure of a black horse on that stone - a dark crystal horse guarding the portal of the stones.

"Maiden Mountain" - The Sleeping Beauty

Chapter 13

'The Sleeping Beauty' Mountain

I have frequently mentioned 'The Sleeping Beauty' mountain. She lies on the East side of Loch Seaforth near the road between Lewis and Harris. When you see her from close by she is utterly stunning. She is so real, so alive, as though she is just about to open her eyes, stir, rise up and walk the earth again. She seems to be one of the Dreamtime ancestors who formed the landscape of these islands.

The most extraordinary thing about her is that when she is viewed from Callanish at the time of the southerly Major Moon Standstill once every 18.6 years, the low moon actually rises from her body as though she is giving birth to the new moon of the next lunar cycle.

Apart from the phenomenon of the mountain being just in the right place, the moon only makes this low skim at this latitude. Further South, even at its lowest, it isn't this low; further north it doesn't rise at all.

The summer after we moved to Lewis was the most recent southerly major moon standstill - 1987. I went to watch every lowest moon that year, even when they were shrouded in cloud. I needed to feel the energies of each of them. The moon's apparent movements are so much more complex than the sun's, and it was a different phase of the moon that got lower through the year until the very lowest was at the end of September - but by then it was the half moon that was low - a half moon for Equinox. The extraordinary moon, the one that had the most powerful energy, was the full moon at its lowest in June.

A group of people gathered to be with me. We sat for several nights watching the moon get lower and fuller until the night of the full moon finally came. The experience of that night really was unlike anything I have ever known: a great cosmic drama between moon and earth: the moon coming to earth, rising, sliding up from the feet of the mountain, up along her legs, her thighs, her belly, then rising slightly above her breasts, her throat...to seemingly pause and look down on her face from so close above almost in an act of love. It was truly very erotic.

Because of the time in 1982 when I had walked the mountain and lay there at her brow, joining with her and the land; on that '87 night, although I sat and watched the event objectively, I also experienced it subjectively as though it were happening to me. It was incredible. The tension and flow of energy between moon and earth/mountain was phenomenal. It was like the birth of a cycle.

As the changing phases of the moon each had their lowest time throughout the year it also seemed as though the lunar energy was rising up though the chakras of the mountain. A time of change. A time of empowerment. I wrote a sequence of poems that summer which were the experiences of the mountain herself as I experienced them.

After the moon has risen from the mountain and moved along her so sensually, it leaves her and disappears behind a rock. A while later it appears again right in the centre of the stones, when viewed from the end of the avenue to the north. To me, the event that matters is the Moon and the Mountain, and having been through the phenomenal experience of that, we didn't feel we could take any more and so my friends and I were already returning to camp when this later event occured. But we weren't allowed to miss it! We were just crossing the end of the avenue on the road when it happened. I was transfixed because suddenly I knew I'd seen all this before, many times before, lifetimes and lifetimes ago - and that people had sat there and watched this phenomenon of moon and mountain long before the stones were put there, and that when they were erected it was done to capture the moon and channel its energy up the avenue - for what purpose? I felt odd about it and always have this slight ambivalence with the stones: much as I love them and feel them to be the ancestors and the grandmothers I am also unsure of the motives of those very knowledgeable Neolithic people in putting them there. What were they doing with that lunar energy?

It brought back the memory of my experience on Windmill Hill in Avebury. Later I wondered how this 'moon in the stones' would have looked when the cairn was in its original state. Would the moon still be visible? Would the moon sit on the top of the cairn? Would it's light and energy be absorbed by the cairn and the contents of the cairn whether they were the dead - spirits waiting to be reborn from the lunar womb-tomb - or the living awaiting the lunar beam of enlightenment before emerging shamanically 're-born' from their dark retreat in the cairn? When the other cairn was discovered beyond the avenue, that seemed to open up a whole other dimension to the beam of lunar light along the avenue.

I find events such as this difficult in some ways. I want to just sit very still and watch and be with place. I want to lose some level of awareness of my surroundings, while at the same time becoming intensely integrated with them. I am quite bothered by swarms of photographers, who are sometimes quite noisy, not actually involved with the event, just intent on getting the best picture of it no matter how much they disturb others - almost as though what they are doing is the most important thing. That evening one photographer even started to set up his tripod right in front of us, completely obliterating our view. I just couldn't believe such lack of understanding or sensitivity to the evening. He muttered and fussed when we complained as though it were us who were in the wrong! The photo matters, not the experience. I was also bothered by groups of people prancing about in costumes, playing recorded music and trying loudly to keep to some event schedule that was going awry. The event was happening in nature. It only happens a few times in a lifetime. You don't have to do anything, you don't have to add anything. I had years before grown out of doing spectacular performances at ancient sites and I'm sure I never imposed anything on other people at a sacred site during such an experience as this. Most of our things were done when we were alone. I just hope that when this event next happens, people will treat it with respect, and also respect the feelings of others who just want to watch it in stillness and quiet. It is enough that it is happening. Just watch and be part of it. Please.

My problem is that I don't own the place either. I don't want to resent other people being there for they have as much right to be there as I, nor do I want them to resent my presence. There seemed to be people there that night in '87 who seemed to resent us just sitting there and trying to watch. There were unpleasant energies around and we went to sit in the cairn to carry out a ritual someone on the other side of the earth had asked us to do and we were asked to leave in a very banal and ridiculous manner. I wouldn't do that again, but our space had already been so intruded on. I hope next time that everyone can be considered and the focus will be to just quietly watch this gift of an experience.

The Mountain is formed by three hilltops: Mor Mhonadh, Guainemol and Sidhean an Airgid. This latter is her head. Airghid means silver - silver at her Brow. This evening in 1987, the low moon was blood red. Maybe in the past, before the climate changed, when the skies were very clear and unpolluted, the low moon was silver and painted the mountain silver also. I certainly felt that night that that silver energy spread out, spiralling and swirling across the land and into our hearts. A group of friends and I refer to the Sleeping Beauty as "Airghid" as though it is her personal name, and I refer to her thus in my poems.

Another remarkable aspect of this mountain is how she changes her shape according to where you view her from. There is another mountain - Beinn Mhor - behind her. As you move along the road from Leurbost to Callanish (from east to west of the island) the mountain behind her alters her apparent shape when you see her from different places. At Achmore, the mountain behind makes her appear pregnant. There is a ridge that runs alongside and higher than the road and at Achmore, up on this ridge are the remains of a Neolithic stone circle. These stones now lie flat in the peat. It is a perfect circle, unlike the other circles of the Callanish complex, and this may mean it is older - it certainly feels like that to me. It feels as though it belongs to an older people than those who built the more spectacular circles. I will come back to this place at Lammas.

At other points on the ridge the mountain appears to be being impregnated or to be giving birth. From Callanish main circle the mountain behind appears to have left her, is beyond her head and no longer part of her body. It seems as though there were specific places from where to view her in different aspects, and they were there to celebrate these physical manifestations of the earth goddess at different times of the cycle of the year.

As you travel from north to south of the island, she also seems to change her appearance. Further north she is rugged and quite ugly. By Loch Seaforth, especially at Arivruach, she is absolutely stunning and like a mature woman. Further south and just before her woman shape begins to disappear altogether, she appears very young and maiden-like. Strangely, although I've only ever heard her referred to in English as 'The Sleeping Beauty', even by Lewis people, apparently in Gaelic she is also known as 'Cailleach na Mointeach' or old woman of the moors. As far as I'm concerned the one thing she never resembles is an old woman! Maybe it refers more to her age in time, for she was lying there long ages before we ever appeared on this earth. There are many legends of Dreamtime Ancestors creating landscape features such as 'The Giantesses Apronful'. These Ancestors are the Old Woman, the Cailleach. Indeed I believe 'The Cailleach Bheure' is credited somewhere with the creation of the Western Isles.

Her body is very smooth, her knees slightly raised, her belly flat, and her two small breasts quite maiden-like. The old woman lies elsewhere. More of her later.

I feel that this mountain, this incredible physical representation of Goddess in the landscape, self-created by nature, with her apparently changing form and relationship with the moon, must be one of the main reasons why so many circles were sited in the Callanish area. That there should be this co-incidence of the moon rising from her body is extraordinary. She must have been worshipped, or at least honoured, for aeons before the stones were erected.

Somehow, I will always belong to this mountain, will always have to keep returning to her, even though I no longer live at her feet.

Chapter 14

Summer and the Solstice

So now we are reaching the height of the summer. On Lewis, the magic of this time was so different from anything I'd known before, and certainly completely unlike England.

For the two months of mid-May to mid-July the sun only just sets, and the skies remain a sort of rainbow-twilight: a kind of blue, green, orange on the horizon: magical colours, like the otherworld, the timeless realm of Faerie, the realms you go to in visions and visualisations. Those things you could do with the time just went on and on and on. I would do a normal day's "things", then at 8 or 9pm go up to the peats and do a couple of hours there, and then still have time to do something else. One summer we went out a lot with a neighbour in a fishing boat on the loch. We'd maybe go out at 10pm and Talie and I would come home at midnight. I'd think - 'we can't sleep in the house on a night like this' and we'd get the sleeping bags and sleep outside. Although I would have had to light candles in the house, I found there was still enough light outside if I wanted to read.

That summer fishing was quite special for me. There were times when I felt like just another animal in a chain. Shoals of fish would come in, moving in extraordinary patterns; the birds would follow the fish and we would follow the birds and find the fish. It was like all of nature working together somehow and with us as part of it, as we always had been.

I maybe need to say here that I've been vegetarian for a lot of my life and am back to being more or less so again. In the

"The Tall Stone - Dancing With Rainbows", Midsummer
Sunset, Callanish

early '80's when I received the Tibetan Dzog Chen teachings I was taught that if I ate an animal with awareness and did a practice for it, I could place a good cause for and benefit that being and at that point I ate meat again, but always with awareness. I realise this, where meat must pass through three pairs of hands before it reaches you, is different from being involved in the death of the animal, but if Talie and I ate fish from the loch we always went later with the head and returned it to the loch and sat in communication with the spirit of the fish, giving our thanks. This is not something I would do in anything but the environment in which we were living.

It was beautiful walking beside that loch of an evening or at night, when it was still and everything else was silent. You would hear the plop, plop of leaping fish and the occasional slow and melancholy flap, flap of a solitary heron.

One thing I wanted to do, never did and still want to do, is travel round the island by boat. I want to see what everywhere looks like from the sea, to approach places like Gravir, like Callanish, from the sea, for they had no roads, those people in the past, even fairly recently, and that was the reality of how it all was to them, coming in from the sea, and every place linked to every other place by the sea rather than the land.

Oh, those magical nights of summer. The first year I was there, in 1982, a group of us went to visit Annie Macleod of Callanish. We talked and talked, then thought it must be getting on, maybe 10pm, and we'd better leave, only to find it was 2am.

I loved to lie in the heather with the bog cotton waving in the breeze all around. It was like Faerieland. There were yellow irises that bloomed everywhere in wet places, like faces of sunshine. When I first lived there I was amazed in the summer when they took the sheep from the roadsides and up onto the common grazings, at how quickly a rich abundance of wild flowers and plants grew by the wayside; silverweed, meadowsweet, tormentil, clover, orchids - and oh, so much more. I always picked a supply of eyebright to see me through the winter, for sometimes the peat dust gave me sore eyes and there's nothing like eyebright for curing it.

Oh, those summer nights! There were years when I was out driving around really late and people were out everywhere, working, at the peatbanks, children playing. What it must have been like when they worked the crofts, out with the crops and animals in the summer, working outside the houses...

The energy was crazy, rising to a kind of crescendo at midsummer. It felt as though anything was possible, the sense of infinite possibility, as though impossible and crazy things really could happen, as though you could make all your dreams come true, work magic, make things happen. Some did happen, but then midsummer would be like a bubble bursting, a balloon deflating; the potential died as the year began to descend.

But hang on, we haven't reached midsummer yet!

Paint the roof, do the peats. When the peats that are lying flat have dried enough on one side to be solid enough to be stood up, you make little piles of five of them - like little dolmens. I used to think dolmens must be the petrified piles of giants' peats drying. As they dried further you'd turn them, then build them up into bigger piles, trying to get the wind to blow onto every peat. It was the wind you wanted to dry them rather than the sun. If the sun dried them on one side too quickly from wet, they'd go all curvy and your perfect peat is of regular size and shape and flat. I didn't have many perfect ones and lots of mine broke into pieces. I always seemed to have as many bags of broken pieces as I had good big square chunky bits.

And so it was midsummer - the Summer Solstice. The peak of the year. The moment when once again time seemed to pause between breaths, the pause at the other end of the pendulum's swing. It was as though all my life in England I'd risen towards the peak and never got there, but here on Lewis it all went on and on and on and further and further and higher and higher and finally we got there at last. Like a kind of cosmic orgasm!

Talie's birthday is June 13, so we always had his party just before going off to Callanish for the Solstice. The year he was 3, he actually woke up on his birthday in the Callanish stones! How often though, his birthday was cold and wet and windy!

In the early years I'd go and camp at Callanish for days - up to the north of the village at the old camp-site where I could sit outside by a small fire all night if I wished. There were never many people gathering for the sunrise then. In the early '80's before I had Talie, I and one or two friends would be the only ones there. With Talie as a young child it got more difficult for me to sit in the stones all night, and the camp was too far from the stones for me to leave him in the tent alone. As the years passed, more and more people would gather for the Solstice. It will never get like Stonehenge, being so far for most people to go, and the journey requiring a great deal of dedication for most who make it. There were so many different people coming for so many different reasons. There are always a few photographers if the sunset or sunrise looks like being a horizon one. Many of them sit in their vehicles with a warm flask and just pop out if there's the chance of a good shot. There are some New Age people with their own agendas, of which I am very suspicious. I am very against 'crystal planting' - the crystals are in the stones already and

I'm sure the people who put the stones there had a much better idea of what they were doing than people do today. I am very opposed to people who seek to change the patterns of energy in the earth.

Some people are there just to gather with others at this special time of year. Some come looking for a Festival, and there isn't one, but they have a good time all the same. So-called Travellers are mostly well-behaved and don't leave any mess. It tends to be city-dwellers 'out in the wilds' who don't know how to behave in the country who make the mess and the Travellers who clear up after them.

There are people like me who just want to be with the stones and experience and mark this special time of year, and there are often, especially if the Solstice is a Friday, lots of "lads" and lasses from Stornoway, in cars, roaring about, looking for a good time and wondering what "the hippies" will get up to. When there are a lot of dubious New Age folk around (and by these I don't mean the Travellers) I always feel the Stornoway lads have more right to be there, even if they do turn up with carry-outs and ghetto-blasters. It's their circle, and maybe in some weird way they are acting as it's guardians.

There are always quite a few local people, who turn up in the night, often barefoot, compelled to go there, not really knowing why, in defiance almost of the Free Church which condemns the place and the stones themselves as Satanic.

It is a wonderful time. To me the most important time is the Solstice Eve. To see the sun set, sit through the shortest night that barely seems like night and see the sun rise onto the longest day is to me perfection. After that the energy seems to wane. I never feel like celebrating on the night of the Solstice. It's over. One year we went to see Annie Macleod on the day of the Summer Solstice and she said "It's the first day of winter today".

I remember one wonderful year when some people I knew camped near the stones and I could leave Talie to sleep in their bender, and I had one of the most wonderful nights of my life. Often people would be exhausted by sunrise and go off to sleep and there wouldn't be that many people actually there to greet the sun. One year, a friend sat on a rock to the south of the stones and said that when the sun rose, the great tall centre stone was like a mirror, reflecting the light of the rising sun. There is a legend that at the midsummer sunrise 'the Shining One' will come up the avenue into the stones.

One year, after the sunrise, still so early, everyone else abed, I sat with one other woman by a fire-side making porridge... It was like the days of the East Anglian Faires in the 70's. Maybe like once it was .... long, long ago ....

Most of the local people I knew didn't mind the visitors, but there were some around not originally from the island who spread a lot of very untrue stories and created some panic and bad feeling. These people were pretty paranoid. Although Caledonian MacBrayne, the ferry company, now seems to ban "Travellers'" vehicles, usually claiming they are carrying Calor Gas cylinders or something, which they aren't allowed to, the people in charge of the place, the police etc., are very sensible and just keep an eye on things and there's very little trouble, if any.

The sad thing for me was when it was decided that the place needed a Visitor Centre. I campaigned for years against this, and I think the campaign raised awareness of the place as something other than a dead monument to be exploited purely for financial gain and also that it wasn't just one circle, but a circle in a sacred landscape.

Eventually a modified plan went ahead and a Centre was built. The building now is actually very pleasant and nestles fairly unobtrusively into the environment, but the car/coach park is lit at night and takes up rather more space than it actually provides parking for. My main concern remains the paths that have been built - both from the Centre to the stones and, even worse, around the stones themselves. These have really spoilt the surrounding area. The one round the stones seriously interferes with the energy of the site, and worst of all, cuts right through the middle of the long avenue to the north. All the reasons given for this, that it's helping stop damage to the site, are in fact rubbish and the Powers-that-be seem unable to see how the path is doing even more damage to the site. If you talk of site 'energy' however, you are regarded as a right crank!

There are a lot of tourist coaches in the summer. All tourists are encouraged to go to Callanish for 10 minutes, no matter how little interest they actually have in the site and this then creates a problem that requires paths and coach parks to solve. Chicken and egg situation. Sort of. It was inappro-priately dressed coach parties allegedly complaining about muddy shoes that caused the paths to be constructed in the first place.

However, after all my campaigning - when the Centre opened, run by local people, the energy of it felt really good. Something had actually shifted over the years, and it seems more 'alright' to appreciate the stones now. I actually felt that some negative energy that had been focussed round the stones had gone.
The stones themselves though, around the height of the summer tourist season, especially in the day, just seem to withdraw their presence and those ancestors, grandmothers, shamanic spirits, go off somewhere else for a bit until it gets less busy. The stones stand there as just stones, looking somewhat smaller.

So, for me, that was the peak, the turn. It was what I had waited for all year, but the joy of such an amazing time was tinged with the sadness that we were now beginning the descent into the darkness again.

I never really had that open-ended freedom to just be with it, just go on enjoying it. There was always the pressure to get back to the roof-painting, back to the peats; and in the latter years, back to making up card orders and doing Craft Fairs in Stornoway. I didn't like to leave my exhibition for too long, either. I was torn between my own need to be at Callanish and the knowledge that this was one of the times of year when the people most interested in my work would be on the island. In the summer I often had to put up exhibition visitors for the night, for if they didn't have a car, there was no means of getting back to Stornoway until the next day. There are more buses now, and a hostel a few miles away.

Part of me longed to spend all summer just being with the stones; but living on the island made that impossible. I still dream that one day I shall live on that amazing road that leads up to the stones, so that I can just walk up there of a sunset or sunrise, or when the moon is dark or full or there's an eclipse. The road itself feels like a processional way and there is a single stone along it at the north of the village. It is not on the same alignment as the avenue and its distant cairn, but strangely, up that way is the Graveyard.

Ah, Callanish, you are in my heart for ever.

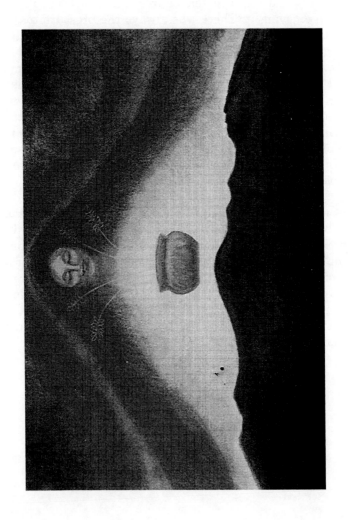

"Lammas Mountain"

Chapter 15

The Peats and Lammas (1st August)

How quickly the summer passed. By the time English people came up for their holidays, it felt as though it were almost Autumn.

It didn't seem long before Lammas - the nights already getting dark, the strange unfamiliarity of having to light candles, lamps and torches again.

Had I been living on the island when I was a child, the crofts would have been properly farmed, the people still living from their own land, their own environment; to a very large extent anyway. How it has all changed. Now there is nothing. In a few townships you'll see people cutting and drying hay, but in many not even this is done any more. When I moved to Gravir, I think 2 - 3 people did it, but they soon died and that was that. Very occasionally you will see an isolated lazy-bed still growing potatoes, but that's very rare.

There is very differing treatment of the sheep. Some people care for their animals very well, feeding them concentrates through the winter, but others, many others, just leave them out, often on the roads, with no extra food, to fend for themselves. Many ewes are in bad condition by the time they lamb and just die from the hardship of trying to survive, and a lot of fleece comes off long before the shearing when animals have been poorly kept. I'm always amazed how little some people bother.

So, come Lammas, there was no sense of 'harvest', of the achievement of getting it all in after the hard work of spring and summer. My own potato crop was nowhere near ready and I'd usually just have one or two tiny ones as a Lammas offering. How easily a few crofts could be 'Improved' and subsidised to keep the island self-sufficient in potatoes, but no-one seems to see the point - so Safeway sells potatoes from Egypt, New Zealand....If only people could think globally and act locally or whatever the saying is...meantime ships chug (or whatever ships do) round the world and juggernauts thunder up and down motorways, irreplaceable fuel gets wasted, asthma in children grows and the world gets warmer....

My own sense of harvest featured The Peats. It is what I had spent my summer doing. All that time; all that physical energy. Often, if the summer weather hadn't been good I would have turned and turned the damp blocks, trying to get them dry, and by the time I got them home I would feel I knew each piece personally. I'd sit by the fire in the winter and I would know which bank each one had come from. Each one was different. In the early days I'd curse the sheep for trampling on them when they were wet, but I've heard that a peat with a sheep's footprint on it used to be highly regarded, maybe some form of luck?

Over the years I developed an intense relationship with the area where my peat banks were. I would go into an almost meditative state up there for hours on my own, and everything became timeless, or maybe of all time. The past seemed very close - with little difference between past and present.

I have found it impossible to deny what seems to be the reality of re-incarnation and 'past lives'. I seem to remember so much, to have so many personal memories of lives before this one. Maybe it is the place that remembers and shares its memories; I'm open to many explanations, but I do actually feel these to be personal memories.

I seem to have many really clear memories of Gravir, and it seems to be why I went to live there - went back; that I had 'unfinished business' to tidy up. Maybe I'll write a novel about all that someday! It's very different from my experience of the stones and other ancient parts of the island. That seems more to do with connecting with other people from the past than with personal memory. I seem to remember the place where my peat banks are as they were long before the peat was there, before the climate changed, when it was a sunlit wood of hazel and silver birch.

Now, when you reach the rock bottom of the peat, there are tree roots, trunks, branches, twigs and hazel nuts. When you come across the branches, they look as though they had only recently fallen. The bark is shiny, the inside strangely red - like blood - so if you cut through one it is like cutting through bone. When they have lain in the sun a while, they dry out and become more fragile. I collected bags and bags of it. I couldn't bring myself to burn it and eventually stopped cutting those banks - they felt too sacred, for this indeed became my own personal sacred site. It seemed as though there were an entrance to the Faerie realm in this place, and I was close to Faerie there. I'd often walk home down the steep curving hill and so much of what I felt would make sense. It seemed like some sort of karma from long distant lives...

I love the physical stuff of peat: it's texture, it's smell...Banks are meant to be kept well-drained, but mine were so higgledy-piggledy that I'd get as much as I could from them once they were turfed, and often I was cutting under water. As I put my hands and arms down into the warm brown water and pulled out a peat, it would seem that the Earth had given birth - and I was her midwife. The peat was the Earth's gift to me for the winter, so the peat was my harvest.

When I first went up to these banks I'd see water covered in oil and I'd think how awful that people dumped stuff in this beautiful environment, but I found out that it is natural - the peat is quite rich in paraffin.

The tractors can drive onto the crofters' banks, so all most of them have to do is pile the peats up onto the banks, but mine were inaccessible and I had to carry them all to the road. We are talking something like 300 sacksful! It certainly kept me fit, and the first year I didn't cut them, when I was preparing to move, I certainly noticed the difference in my body.

The first years, I paid some-one with a tractor and trailer to take them home for me and then would have to build a peat-stack outside the house. In latter years, when I had the car, I'd put them all in salmon-feed sacks and take them home myself, load after load after load. It would take me until late September.

I saw a change in those 10 years I lived there; not only from the wonderful craft of peat-stack building to the increasing piles of salmon-feed sacks, but in attitude. When I moved there, people who didn't cut peat were looked down on; by the time I left, with more and more people going over to "the oil", the peat-cutting itself was looked down on by many: "Oh, do you still do peats?" they'd say, as though it were a thing of the past and only those who were poor and especially unemployed, had the time to be out there on the moors at the peats. How fast tradition dies!

I rejoiced in my peat harvest and I'd take some small pieces with me when Talie and I would go to celebrate Lammas at the stone circle at Achmore that I've mentioned before. In the early years, we'd spend the night there; us and the mountain - and the midges. The midges are another story. If you've not met a Highland midge, you've not lived. What are they for in nature's cycle of things? I have heard that bats eat them so I had this fantasy that I could have a hat with a team of trained and tethered bats flying around, eating the midges and keeping them off me. They get you into mental states like that, I can tell you!! When I first moved there, I thought you must get immune with time, then I met an old lady on the road, all wrapped up in headscarves, saying "Aren't the midges terrible tonight?" and I despaired.

I was sort of allergic to them and would go all funny and cold and ill-feeling when I was bitten and my face would swell up terribly and I'd look as bruised as if I'd been in a fight...

Achmore: it doesn't look much now with the stones lying flat where they've been discovered in the peat, but the ancient circle is on a kind of plateau on a hill-side, and there in front of you, filling the horizon is the profile of the pregnant Harvest Mother. The Mother Goddess indeed. I can think of no other reason why that stone circle should be sited there, but to honour, celebrate and revere this physical manifestation of She who provides, at the time of her Great Harvest. It is like a ceremonial viewing platform with the mountain herself as the cosmic performance. We would bring our little gifts and offerings and often a 'corn dolly' made of grass and reeds from our garden, for we had no grain crops. I'd bring a few ears of wheat or barley from our visits to England with which to decorate her. We just had this enormous sense of gratitude, me and my young son, giving thanks for everything we had, for the health of each other, and the carrots, potatoes and peat that would see us through the long dark winter.

We'd sit there at sunset and watch her profiled against the darkening sky; sometimes there would be a still lowish full moon above her. We would feel very connected to other harvest places, like Silbury Hill in Wiltshire, and the people celebrating there.

Once we had the car, we'd usually go on to the main Callanish circle. My Australian friend, Lynne Wood, had pointed out to me how when you look at the stones in profile, they seem to echo the form of the pregnant Sleeping Beauty, and so it is. The tall central stones rise up as her belly, and of course, there in the centre is the burial cairn - the womb-tomb of the stones.

My Leo birthday is August 9, and sometimes our harvest/Lammas celebration would also celebrate that. The last birthday I had on the island was one of the lovliest of my life. Three friends - Rita, Anne and Wendy, joined me and Talie. We walked a labyrinth to give gifts to a corn dolly in the centre and then we feasted while there was the most wonderful deep orange sunset. Times like that will stay with me for ever - the epitome of my ecstasy of being with that incredible island.

For other birthday/Lammas times I might go to Bosta beach on the island of Great Bernera. This is now joined to Lewis by a bridge. I regard Bosta as a very special and sacred site. When I first went to Callanish in 1982, I slept one night in Circle III. One dream there was amazing and showed me where the stones for the Callanish circles had come from. A few days later I went to Bosta for the first time and recognised it as the place in the dream. Friends I was with went off independantly, and when we met up they were very excited, having been convinced by the rocks there that this was where the stones had come from. (I hadn't really told them about the dream). No theories will convince me otherwise, I'm afraid. The stones could have been taken round by water to the eventual circle site. Other theories suggest they came from a quarry, but I think it is completely against how these people would have functioned in the world to quarry rock.

Bosta just feels like an incredibly sacred place. Recently the battering of the winter seas began to reveal remnants of ancient occupation there and when it was excavated, ruins of an Iron Age settlement were found. The last I heard, I believe they think there are even older remains lower down. It seemed to confirm everything I felt about the place, and when I heard that people believe there is something ancient beneath a modern cemetary there, it seemed to affirm what I had seen in my dream.

Sometimes you can be alone there with the sheep and cattle who come to wander the beach and eat seaweed. At other times there are many visitors, both tourists and local people - especially on Sundays, when they aren't meant to do anything except go to church and read the Bible. They escape to Bosta, thinking they'll only be seen by others doing the same. It's also a place where lads and lasses (and their cars) congregate of an evening.

Before I lived up there, I went to Bosta in the summer of 1983 and I slept on the beach, thinking I would have the place completely to myself. Quite early in the morning I found myself surrounded by the local school having their Sports Day!

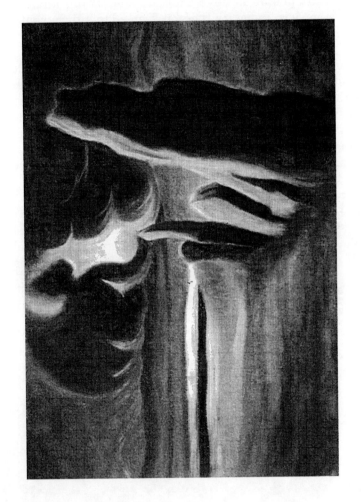

"Catching the Last Rays", Equinox Sunset, Callanish

Chapter 16

Autumn Equinox
(Around 21st September)

Now the year is really turning down to winter again. At this time of year on Lewis there will sometimes be something almost like winter, and then summer will briefly return again. It can become very dynamic and changeable - rain and dark skies followed by golden sunshine, creating many rainbows and unbelievably rich colours when gold and orange sunlight hits the hillsides and the Callanish stones.

Although there isn't what I recognise as Autumn as in England, the colours of the Hebridean landscape are very rich at this time of year. The bracken is a deep orange; the heather which has been purple when in bloom now becomes a deep rich reddish-brown - a colour I have seen nowhere else. The grass becomes brilliant green and orange when wet. The Stones themselves change from white to deep pink, deep orange and I have even seen them blue! I don't think there is any colour that I haven't seen those stones turn, even green.

So we would go to the Callanish main circle again, to be with the Callanish Dance once more. Turning to the winter half of the year instead of the summer. Turning from the light to the dark. The stone which had shown herself to me as Eostara, goddess of spring, now appeared as a hooded figure facing the other way - facing the north and winter. The rising sun seemed to enter her belly, as though she then held it in her womb through the winter to give birth to it once more in spring.

There was usually a very peaceful energy at Callanish at Autumn Equinox. There was the sense of this brief moment in time to look back on the summer - its joys, its achievements, and some of its wild energies; and to look forward with deep contemplation to that long winter to come. There was almost something of a sense of relief from so much light, so much sun, that other extreme; the feeling that at this half-way time everything was a bit more normal and we could relax a little before the extreme of dark. The stones themselves maybe relaxed a little after the onslaught of so many tourists' feet. There's the sense that they shouldn't so much be looked at, as looked from or looked through; as though the focus of attention is wrong. The path turns them into something like an ornamental garden to be stared at, and everything is a bit out of balance.

At this Equinox time I would appreciate and give thanks for the amount of light we still had, knowing how soon it would be gone.

Sometimes, at other parts of the island, the energies would not be so serene. It brought home to me how the cycles of our lives echo the cycles of the year, the cycles of nature. I didn't realise I had been going through my menopause until it was almost over. I didn't have a physical menopause in the sense of all the symptoms many women suffer. I had an emotional one. I suffered great extremes of emotion and my normal ability to deal with emotional things completely left me and everything totally freaked me out. I couldn't cope with the most ordinary everyday things of life - in fact these were some of the most difficult to deal with. It was like having a breakdown. It was like being ill. I suppose because I was living in a place so different from where and how I'd lived the rest of my life and because there was so much that was extreme about it anyway, I didn't recognise it as the condition it was until I began to emerge from it. I suddenly began to feel I was 'getting better', recovering from a sickness I hadn't realised I'd had. Unsupported and unhelped - aren't we nearly all? Treated by those around me as a joke, a laugh, a totally panic-stricken human being incapable of doing anything - and all I needed was a little understanding, a little help, a little love and a little cuddle now and again. No wonder I so often ran from other humans and found refuge with the stones.

One Autumn Equinox I went to Bosta Beach and I truly recognised the Kali aspect of the Goddess and of nature as part of ourselves. It was an immense understanding for me of myself, of all women, and of Goddess and Nature herself. I don't believe in a "Goddess" who is all sweetness and light and gentleness - as she is so often portrayed by the New Age. That is only one aspect of her - and of us. I do not think we should deny our own anger and even feelings of violence - as long as we don't let those feelings control us, take us over and cause harm to others. To deny these feelings can be to turn them in on ourselves and result in disease such as cancer. I think it needs to be dealt with in a different way. My Dzog Chen teachings were helpful in this. There is a way of integrating with anger so that it doesn't control us any more.

I think it is wrong to deny the 'anger', 'cruelty' and 'violence' of nature. This is like personifying something which is just part of how things are. It is what is, and is part of the energy of the universe. It is perhaps part of our resposibility as humans - part of our purpose? - to recognise and deal with the anger and violence in ourselves and others. I feel that if we don't recognise it as an just another energy and use it constructively, then it becomes destructive. I believe it can be turned into a creative force, a force for change. I don't agree with the New Age denial of anger. Repression and denial are dangerous. Anger can be very useful as long as it doesn't take us over or go round in circles getting nowhere.

Maybe this was for me the teaching of the Wild Hag, who I truly met at this time of year, at this time of my life and acknowledged as part of my self.

Another teaching I received at Autumn Equinox was about getting my priorities right. Often we would be sitting with Annie Macleod, who was by now quite ill, sometimes quite frightened and lonely. Sitting by her fireside drinking tea I would realise there was about to be a spectacular sunset at the stones, but I would realise that the stones and the sunsets and probably we ourselves would be there long after Annie was gone, and I would stay with her and miss the sunset. When she died aged 79, my shock was profound, my loss great, and when I sat by her grave in the churchyard down by the loch, I was so relieved that there had been those times when I hadn't gone to see the sunset, when I had stayed with Annie.

Growing up with old people, I have a lot of understanding of them, and I loathe this culture of youth which has no time for its elders, despising them, relegating them to poverty and the scrap heap, treating them as stupid and child-like, patronising them, even though most of them never become senile, just frightened and anxious. Instead we should revere them for their knowledge and wisdom, as our ancestors did and as many other cultures still do. Annie shared many of her feelings and fears with me and I feel privileged at that.

I don't think one's spirit, one's 'self' ages at all, at least not in one lifetime. When I think of my earliest memory (age 1 or 2) I am the same person, the same self. I don't seem any younger than now, just frustrated at being in a young body and being treated like a child. When I'm 95 I don't expect my 'self' to feel any older. I'll just be the same me, frustrated now at being in an old body and once again treated as a child. Why don't we treat old people as people, with respect for their life's experience instead of patronising them in their so-called 'second childhood'. What a profound insult. Senility is a disease, but most old people don't suffer from it.

So, having spent once again the night and day of the Equinox with the stones, with candles, incense and aspen leaves honouring the point on the circle of the year, I think the Autumn Equinox is for me a time of teaching, a time to look back on the lessons of the year and life and to prepare to batten down the hatches for Winter.

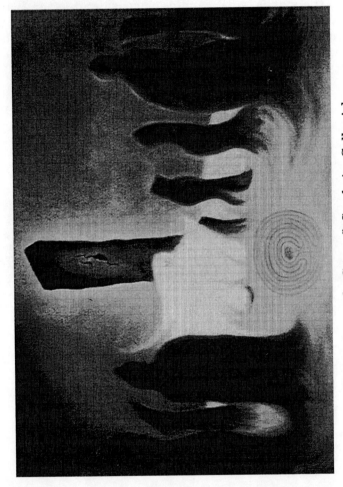

"Returning to the Source", Samhain, Callanish

Chapter 17

Samhain (31st October/ 1st November) and the approach to the depth of winter

I missed that English season - that autumnal approach to winter. In England I love it when the leaves have fallen from the trees; when they start to rot back to earth to feed the roots and the life of the forest floor. I love the dank, pungent smell of that decomposing. I love the stillness that comes with the chill on the air of the first frosts. I love the smell of bonfires and burning Autumn leaves in parks and gardens. I missed the changing autumn colours as the leaves fell from the trees and the crunch of their crispness under foot and the way they swirled in eddys with those first hints of autumn winds. I missed all that.

It was the light that changed on Lewis. I was really shocked at my first Samhain there, for the day was as long then as at midwinter in England - or so it seemed, and there was still so far to go into the darkness and then come out even to this point once more in the new year. It was already profoundly winter, and so long, so very long before the light came again.

Sometimes I would be away in England at this time - to get a touch of Autumn, to ease the length of winter a bit, but as often I wouldn't be away, I would be there, deep in the deepening.

Samhain. The Celtic New Year. The eve of Samhain, the sunset, would be the end of one year and the beginning of the next. The dark of the day, the dark of the year; begin with the dark, the birth of the new from the dark. Samhain. That incredible night when all the doors are open between worlds. Really open. When we can be so close, so very close, to the ancestors. When time pauses for a moment and seems to cease to exist. Past, present, future - it's all one moment. The ancestors are with us, and the doors are open to the realms of Faerie and other beings in which I truly believe, and who I believe share our space, but occupy some other dimension of our space - or should I say we occupy (and maybe intrude on) theirs, for surely they were here before us.

I do find it an extraordinary night and it was even more extraordinary to spend it at Callanish. How wrong, how misguided, are those who call these times evil, of the devil - these concepts are the creations of Christianity seeking to overturn the old religions. This was simply a very powerful and very potent time. It is up to us how we use this power and potency - for understanding and wisdom - or misuse it; or just ignore it, which is like turning away from opportunity, turning one's back on a gift from other realms.

If I was aware of the ancestors at Callanish at other times of the year, how much more so it was at Samhain. The stones seemed to close in, the circle become smaller, the stones taller, and even more alive. They seemed very caring, but only if they felt their lessons would be heard. I always felt they wouldn't suffer fools at all.... I had the sense of their ancientness even more than usual. I could understand the timespan of 5,000 years and I could feel a time even more ancient than that from when the spirits of these stones seem to come.

I would go into the cairn. Physically walk in and down, and I would be in the earth, in the mystic cave for winter. Then I seemed to split. My spirit, my psyche, went deeper and deeper into that meditative hibernation, while the 'outer' bit of me struggled to cope with the unnatural 'busy-ness' of the modern world.

It hit me as it never quite had before - how Samhain is still celebrated as 'Bonfire Night'. In the early years on Lewis, we'd go to a neighbour's house in Gravir for a small garden bonfire and fireworks would flare and scream across the still, silent darkness of the loch.

And then we'd go to Callanish, for there they have a gigantic bonfire on a hill to the north of the village, overlooking part of Loch Roag. They make their bonfire of modern rubbish: tyres, car batteries, furniture, who knows what, and one year it was lit with an explosion of what I can only assume was petrol. It belched rolls of pollution into the air, but when the glorious blaze had died down, when the fireworks were over and the villagers had gone, we'd go to stand by the seething embers and the colours of the flickering flames were amazing - green, turquoise, blue, purple. The wonderful remnant of past ritual celebration mingled with the horror of modern pollution. I used to think of the visual beauty of the mushroom cloud - beauty in the ultimate horror.

I used to find it quite bizarre that in this land of the Free Church of Scotland, the most extreme form of Presbyterianism, the children and teenagers celebrate Hallowe'en, dressing up and going 'trick-or-treating'. Maybe in making a joke of it all, ridiculing it all, they seek to negate any of the true Samhain energies that might still stir in this Celtic people.

As well as Callanish, there were other places that called to us for Samhain. On South Harris, there is another sleeping woman mountain. She is known to local people as an asexual 'giant' I believe, but to friends of mine, people I know, (incomers, visitors) who know this mountain well, she is known as the Hag Mountain. She lies there etched against the skyline, her old woman's face with sharp nose and sunken mouth, scraggy neck and bony ribcage with prominant nipple. She is extraordinary and so powerful. She 'guards' a path which crosses from east to west of the island. The graveyard was on the west when the people lived on the western fertile machair lands, but when the landowners turned the people off so they could put sheep on the land and the people had to try to make a living from the infertile rocky eastern shores, they still carried their dead back across the island to the old graveyard, walking by this 'death road'. So she, the Hag, watches over her dead as they pass. There are flat stones along the way on which the coffins were rested. There are cairns and circles of stones which were also stopping places. It is incredible to walk it. It is very silent, enclosed, sheltered from the winds - and nowadays very boggy! Once you get used to it you can see where the old track was - a very straight raised 'road' with a ditch on either side, now crossed again and again by streams, but visible as raised clumps of heather. We used, when we could, to go to be with her around Samhain time. A powerful experience.

Just before we moved from the island, back to England, we were visited by sculptor Gaye Allen, and with her we walked the Hag Mountain and discovered she has unimagined secrets, not visible from the surrounding land. I won't tell you what they are - you must make the great pilgrimage yourselves if you really want to know!

One Samhain we joined with a group of people and had a bonfire in the centre of a maze drawn on a beach. Into the fire we threw all the 'stuff' we didn't want in our lives and also our hopes for the coming year. I always try to find a fire somewhere to do this for Samhain - to get rid of the baggage, the dross, but also to give thanks for what's been good. The beach was incredible once it was dark. The sand became black and the blood-red embers swirled across it, blown by the wind. The tide would come in over the sand, in the wind, to take the fire of wood and peat, it was all of the elements coming into their power and blending into one. We had walked into the maze in the light and realised in this deep black darkness, we couldn't see our way out! Would we have to stay there till dawn, until next year? or just leave and still 'be in' the centre until we could make another maze to walk out? Somehow we managed to trace the path holding a torch low to the ground - and we got out!

So deep, deep, down and down we go again into the silent, still depths of winter.

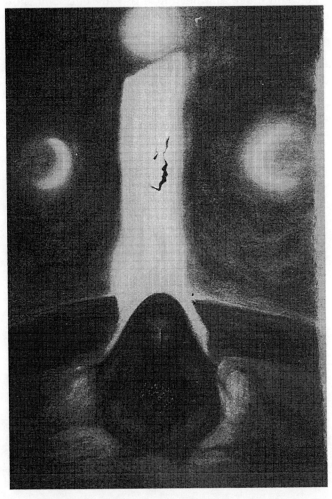

"Of Dark and Light", Midwinter, Callanish

Chapter 18

Winter Returns

And so, once again, we return to winter and the deep, dark, still and silent time of the Solstice. Year after year. Lifetime after lifetime. It seems.

As the years passed on Lewis I became more used to the winter; sometimes it even seemed to pass more quickly than I wished - an impossible thought in the early years. There were things I wanted to get done in the winter: writing, organising paperwork that got chucked here, there and everywhere in the rush and bustle of summer; things I would have no time for once the light began to grow. Sometimes it was just time to think that I needed.

As I developed the business side of my work more: selling prints and cards, doing craft fairs, making up orders for shops, there was even less time for the contemplation of winter. I relaxed into the weather more. The wind had to be much worse to keep me awake at night. The days and weeks flew more quickly by and sometimes, when the light started to grow, much as I welcomed it in one way, it was with a tinge of regret. Dark can be like a comfort blanket: you snuggle down and the dark is like a great mother, making it all better, protecting you from everything difficult and challenging. When the light comes, you're on your own again, facing the harsh realities of life. Nights can be full of demons - mine often are, but there was much I snuggled down into and was loathe to let go of in that darkness of winter.

I was so financially badly off most of the time I lived there and poverty is so crippling and so destructive. It breaks the spirit, and over the years I lost all my strength and sense of self and could hardly believe the life that I'd led before I lived on the island was real. Where had "I" gone? It seemed I had become the person other people saw me as or wanted me to be, as though they could think another me into existence and I was powerless to preserve the real me. Frightening. I'd never had much money all my adult life, but things had never seemed as bad as this and never had such a destructive effect on me.

However, in the latter years of living there, my work brought me in just enough extra money to make me feel more in control of my life and to feel that my real 'self' was returning. I was more able to stock up with all I needed for the winter, so that a week when the weather or whatever cut us off from normality wasn't so traumatic.

My poor, dear car freaked me out a lot of the time. Would it start? What would I do if it didn't? Would it break down? How could I get it fixed if it did? It was a source of constant anxiety, and yet I couldn't have done without it. It gave me some control back, gave me some of my own power back. I found it very difficult to go to town (25 miles each way) only once a week - to have to think of everything and get everything done in one day, often having to go round and round in circles getting nowhere, nothing being at all straightforward, often getting to the point where, even though I hadn't got everything done, I'd just give up because I simply couldn't cope with doing any more - it would just have to wait until next time. I'm someone who likes to go out and do a little bit, return to base, digest what I've done, consider what I've got to do next and then go out and do another little bit. I've never really 'recovered' from the patterns of functioning that come from living nearly the first four decades of my life in London. I found it hard having to plan so far ahead, especially with work things. Doing a paste-up for a small booklet for example, would take weeks instead of a few days, because I just had the one trip a week to get bits of photocopying, especially reductions, done, and then back to do another bit of pasting up and then another week's wait...

A lot of all this stress was just from having to cope with it all on my own - all on my own with the responsibility for a young child. There was no-one to share the burdens or the joys with, no-one to help or support me, no let up from the responsibility. There was a kind of desolation underlining even the best times that I've never really experienced anywhere before or since, not to quite such an extent anyway.

In the winter I'd drive home in the dark, often in rain and wind, sometimes dicing with ice, blinded by oncoming cars, always in danger from the sudden dash across the road by a sheep; then I'd struggle up the slippery garden (no path), through the half-broken gate, and into the dark house. The cats thought they were the most important things in the universe, of course, and clamoured to be fed, but I had to hold a torch and find the matches to light all the candles and oil lamps and the Calor Gas fire. I learned long ago to position matches and candles so I knew exactly where they all were in the dark and could always get the first one lit. It all required a lot of planning in the hours of light and all had to be set up in the morning before I went out.

After this I'd then have to struggle back to the car four or five times in the dark and rain and wind, often gale force, slipping and sliding in the mud, struggling with bags and bags and boxes and boxes of shopping. On my own. It would be at least three quarters of an hour before I could collapse on my bed, read the paper and have something to eat and loads of cups of tea and drinking chocolate. I would already have heated up some meal for Talie. I probably wouldn't have eaten or even had a cup of tea all day. I used to get very bitter. I was more than envious of people who swanned home from their day's shopping into a house full of light, to sit by a warm fire already lit, and have a hot meal brought to them. People would say I had made my choices, but I had never chosen such lonliness, and ten years of this was not what I had expected.

Writing this in late 1997, it astonishes and disgusts me to hear a Labour Prime Minister describe the life of a single mother as 'sitting around all day just waiting for the Benefit cheque to arrive'. I would like him to try living like that for a decade on the money that I had!

Chapter 19

The Circle Turns..... and can I think of leaving.....?

My story could end as we go into the depths of winter again, but this story is a circle and a circle has no end. The end of one thing is the beginning of the next. I turned the circle...over...and over...and over...ten years on that, my beloved island, standing each Winter Solstice with those my beloved stones; my Ancestors, my Teachers, my Grand-mothers; and the circles were deeply, deeply etched into my self, my spirit, my being; but within the circles things do change, things do move on, there have to be shifts in the patterns within the circles, the circles which are maybe a spiral...

And so, as I came near the end of a decade, I knew that there were things in our life which had changed and that because of this, there was going to have to be physical change. I knew we were going to have to leave.

Many people have asked my reasons why. Many people were very surprised that I could even contemplate leaving, knowing how bound I was to that land, to those stones, to that mountain....

I shall never cease to be spiritually bonded to that sacred landscape, but like a child that must leave its mother and go off into the world to live its own life, I realised I must go off to live mine. I had run to the island like running (back?) to Mother, when it was the only place that had seemed like

"Spirits of Pairc Dreaming", Gravir, Isle of Lewis

home; but during those ten years a lot had got sorted out and my strength was coming back; my strength and my power and at last I was my 'self' again, perhaps more my 'self' than ever before.

That island, those stones, that mountain; and Brighde herself - for she is not all gentleness; is the harshness of winter passing as much as the calm of spring coming - had challenged me beyond imagination. It was all extremes there - like the agony and the ecstasy. My spiritual life took me to heights of bliss, serenity and joy, but aspects of my more 'ordinary', 'down to earth' life threw me into the pit of hell and tore me apart. It was like the substance of the island itself - the crystal rock of the Lewisian Gneiss; it was like the weather, like the wind, like the raging sea crashing on the rocks. There was no middle path, no cosy 'middle of the road'. It seemed the heights had to be paid for by the depths. So with the Goddess. No middle path. She gives ecstasy, joy, bliss and serenity, but we are denying half of life if we deny her wildness, her passion, her anger, and that power that can indeed seem like cruelty.

Part of me felt I needed a break from these extremes, a rest from the battering of body and spirit. I knew I now needed a time of being with the less challenging rolling green-ness of parts of England. I knew I needed to be closer to more people that I knew, people of 'like mind'.

When I first moved to the Islands, I became very anti-English; ashamed of what the English had done to the Scottish people, and acutely aware of how London - (or at best Glasgow or Edinburgh-) oriented the media, and the Government are.

I became very Scotland-focussed, and indeed still am to a certain extent, missing Radio Scotland and still reading the *Daily Record*.

But after some years passed, I took back my Englishness, no longer felt prepared to carry the sins of a certain class and certain part of English society. I felt that a very long time back my own ancestors had been as badly treated by such a class. The medieval serf in England had a terrible lot, and more recently the Enclosures were a criminal act against the common people. I ceased to deny the land of my birth. I knew I still had ancient links with areas like Wiltshire and also that Glastonbury in Somerset had always felt like my second home.

None of it was 'reasons'. The move had to happen and lots of things slotted into place like explanations; maybe things 'allowing' me to go, making it easier for me. These became like reasons, but even on that level it was the sum total of many little things, none of which alone were great enough to have made me want to leave. I did not want to leave; it was almost as if the easiest thing was to stay, but that was the easy way out, running away from the challenge, denying all the exciting possibilities that the future might hold for me. A few years earlier, to have left would have been to run away, now it was staying that was.

As far as my work, my art, was concerned, I felt I was just bashing my head against a brick wall on Lewis. I was never going to get anywhere, no further than I already had, anyway. The Arts on Lewis and Harris are run by a small band of "Stornoway Glitterati" who were never going to take me into their clique. They had an image of me which was never going to be shifted. They regarded me and my work as a joke. They had never had any interest in all I had done before I came to the Island nor ever gave me any opportunity to show the skills and potential I had aquired over those years. If I sound bitter, I'm sorry, but I am. As many who's work comes into a spiritual, earth mysteries or Goddess field will know, our work does not fit into the norms of the Art-world, not even of women's or feminist art. I find it sad that galleries in places like Stornoway strive to compete with the Art-world of London and to become like them and turn their back on work which comes from the very spirit of the land. I also seemed to be unacceptable because I hadn't come through a conventional Art School training, the experience of life apparently counting for nothing.

I knew that my work was valued elsewhere, indeed I had already sold a fair amount of original art-work to people on mainland Scotland, in England, the Continent, Australia and the USA. I felt I must go to where it was easier to get it out to the people who wanted it.

It was enough for me, in the end, that my cards sold well at the Loch Erisort bookshop in Stornoway and at the Callanish Visitor Centre, and I was told they were 'well received' in the Callanish village, which meant a lot; that they would sell well to young girls who came to my Craft Fair stall in the Town Hall in their school lunch breaks. That all felt like a great achievement.

My beautiful exhibition space in Gravir was so far from the tourist trail and only a few valiant souls would make their way down there each year, though, as I have said, my work spread from there around the world. It was also very comforting that by the time I left, quite a lot of my original work had found safe and appreciative homes on the Island.

I had to stay to see the opening of the Callanish Visitor Centre in 1995. Although I had campaigned so long and hard against it, I warmed to the form it eventually took, though I still wish I could do something about the paths round the stones. To have left before this opened would have been to have run away. I had to stay through the great 'Calanais' exhibition which was staged in 3 parts by the An Lanntair Gallery in Stornoway, even though, after ten years dedication to the stones I was not asked to participate in the smallest way in exhibition, catalogue or CD. It took a great deal of strength, but to have left before this would also have been running away.

General attitudes towards me seemed to change a bit towards the end. I received help from Western Isles Enterprise; I was for a while Secretary of the Outer Hebrides Crafts Association; I served briefly on the local Community Council and for much too short a while before I left was a volunteer Fire Fighter on the South Lochs unit. (In such a place as the Islands, the Brigade is much to be praised for actively recruiting women fire fighters.)

There came the point when I had the sense of finished business, though only time will tell exactly what. Maybe as I write more and explore the depths of my experience I will come to understand something of what went on.

There were many little things coming at me from all sides: the changes in the bus time-tables (I still often had to use the buses) which I found unacceptable; the increasing street lights and consequent light pollution of the beautiful darkness of Gravir; the South Lochs 'motorway' ploughing through hill and loch; the worsening battle to keep the sheep from my garden - even trees that had struggled for ten years got destroyed in the end; - the battle to keep the building together with no money and no help; even being surrounded on all sides by caravans so that at certain times of year there was nowhere I could sit in my garden without being overlooked....many more little things.... the lack of any colour photocopier on the island making it increasingly difficult for me to complete the card orders I was building up and the amount of time I was spending on this development in my work meaning I had less time to do the peats, paint and repair the house....

Things had changed. What I was doing had changed. Priorities had changed and my needs in the living of daily life had changed. It was time to go. My son was nearly a teenager and needed a different life. I needed a different environment.

I set the plan in action. I told the Universe what I needed to happen - what was going to happen. I advertised my beloved house in many places and got a great deal of interest and response, but it was a small card in the window of a charity shop at the top of Glastonbury High Street which brought my dream family to Gravir to take over our home - not to tear it down and build a breeze-block kit house, but to cherish it as we had done and be able to look after it better than I.

In August 1996, with my daughter Saffron once more helping us, we drove a Luton van from Glastonbury to Gravir, and after over six months of bonfires, trips to dumps, charity shops and sales, packed up our remaining possessions and drove off the island.

I weep to write these words, for my heart and spirit still belong to that Island and always will, and I shall return and return and return, and maybe, who knows, one day I shall go back to live there, but it will be knowing what I do now, and it will be to live in a different way and it will not be to live in Gravir.

I need to integrate the different bits of my life: the sacred and the profane maybe, the spiritual and the mundane perhaps.

I want to end this story with two poems; the first I wrote as I began to realise that I would have to leave, although I was still emotionally torn...........

And Can I Think of Leaving.......?

And can I think of leaving
this my home...?
and can I think of leaving
this my love...?

I The storm is raging
and after the storm will come silence
and the rush of the swollen river
and the trickle of clear water
over wet peat sparkling...
 and can I think of leaving
 this my home...?

II The bird is singing
and after the song will come sweetness
and the warmth of the sun on my skin
and the blue of the sky
and the touch of a breath
that carries like honey
a caress on the air
 and can I think of leaving
 this my home...?

III The evening is long ...
and turns to dawn
with no dark of night
and I can sleep
on heather and stone
by cotton-grass waving
dream of faerie
and shiver at the snipe...
 and can I think of leaving
 this my home...?

IV The midges bite
and drive me home
from the still peat banks

where the fuel dries
for the dark winter fires,
fruit of our summer
labour of long hours...
and can I think of leaving
this my home...?

V The days are shrinking
the nights are growing
rainbows arch
through sun and rain
purple heather,
orange grass
colours rich
 change as we pass...
 and can I think of leaving...
 this my home...?

VI The nights are chilling
still water in the loch
herons flapping
fish flopping
vast black skies
with galaxies turning
 and can I think of leaving
 this my home...?

VII My heart is breaking
my spirit aching
my dreams are dying
the circle complete
The years are passing
and time is running......
out........
 and I must think of leaving
 this my home...
 and I must think of leaving
 thee my love...

Winter 1994/95

The second I wrote not long before I left - one summer's day,
when Talie went off on a trip with the Young Archaeologists
and I went on my own to Callanish, where I sat by the stones
in the warm summer wind and sunlight and I wrote......

The roof fell in on Annie's house at last.
Year after year the wild gales and winter storms
tore and lashed at the sagging thatch,
and then, at last, as she had done,
it gave up the struggle.

Now the doors have gone
and the windows too,
and the old brass bedstead standing crooked
with grass and flowers growing through -
exposed not only to the weather
but the curious eyes of every passing stranger.
Not long now before the house itself
will crumble to a ruin
indistinguishable from the rest.

So does the present become history
and show us the transience of it all.

The trees still grow
in what was once her garden
but the roof has fallen in
on Annie's house at last.

Down in the graveyard
where the earth
thrusts itself into the sky
there is silence
and birdsong
and the peewit's call
and the rustle of long grasses
in the heat of the summer breeze,
and the sea - always present -
sparkling in the sun.

The moment that was Annie
will last for ever
like the memory of a breath
somewhere
re-playing for eternity,
still to be entered
though everything else moves on
and the roof on Annie's house
has fallen in at last.

The roof on Annie's house has fallen in at last -
now I can leave
carrying the spirit of this place
wherever I go
until it is time
for me -
to return once more
maybe for my own eternity......

July, 1996

Blessed Be, Lewis, you will be in my heart for ever.....

Jill Smith in the Callanish Stones,
photo by Suzanne Harris

Place Names

Throughout this book I have used the English spellings for place names in the Western Isles. This is because, writing in English, it seems more fitting to use the English rather than Gaelic, and to use Gaelic when one is writing in Gaelic. Also, many of the names now in Gaelic were originally Norse from when the Vikings owned the Islands, so it seems a bit too politically correct to turn everything into Gaelic, but it is a sensitive issue, as the Islanders suffered so much at the hands of the English and nowadays they are trying very hard to save Gaelic from becoming a dead language. However, for those inspired by this book to visit the Islands, you will find the road signs are in Gaelic, so here is a list of names I mention in both languages. It is worth getting a Gaelic-English dictionary to help you with pronounciation as the Gaelic is so different from English, French etc and can be confusing. For example Callanish is Calanais, which actually sounds like Callanish and not "Callanay" as one might think if one is used to French spelling.

Lewis	-	Leodhas
Harris	-	Na Hearadh
Stornoway	-	Steornabhagh
Tarbert	-	Tairbeart
Gravir	-	Grabhair
Callanish	-	Calanais
Leurbost	-	Liurbost
Achmore	-	Acha Mor
Linshader	-	Linsiadar

Great Bernera	-	Bearnaraigh
Bosta	-	Bostadh
Melbost Borve	-	Mealabost, Borgh
Rodel	-	Rodil or Roghadal
Macleod stone	-	Clach Mhicleoid
Peewit Hill	-	Druim nan Curracag
Arivruaich	-	Airidh a Bhruaich

I trust I have these correct. I was unable to get a list of placenames from the Western Isles Tourist Board, so have taken them from an old map or from other bits of information I have.

Not So Much a Bibliography, More a Suggested Reading, or Rather 'Books That Have Inspired Me Over the Years and Which You May Also Enjoy'

ALLIONE, Tsultrim. *"Women of Wisdom"* Routledge and Kegan Paul. 1984.

APULEIUS, Lucius. *"The Golden Ass"* (trans.Robert Graves)Penguin. 1950.

BALASKAS, Janet. *"Active Birth"*. Unwin. 1983.

BARNES, Richard. (Ed.) *"The Sun in the East"*. R.B.Photographic. 1983. (CONTAINS ARTICLE BY AND PHOTOGRAPHS OF JILL WHEN STILL JILL BRUCE.)

BELL, Andrew. *"Spirit Level"*. Private Publication. 1980.

BELL, Diane. *"Daughters of the Dreaming"*. McPhee Gribble/ George Allen and Unwin. 1983.

BORD, Janet and Colin. *"A Guide to Ancient Sites in Britain"*. Paladin. 1979

BUTTON, John. (Ed.) *"The Best of Resurgence"*. Green Books. 1991.(CONTAINS ARTICLE BY JILL SMITH ON 'SALMON'.)

CAMERON, Anne. *"Daughters of Copper Woman"*. Press Gang. 1981.

CARMICHAEL, Alexander. *"Carmina Gaedelica"*. Floris Books. 1992.

CASTLE, Leila. (Ed.) *"Earth Walking Sky Dancers"*. Frog. 1996.(CONTAINS CONTRIBUTION BY JILL SMITH.)

COOPER, J.C. *"An Illustrated Encyclopaedia of Traditional Symbols"*. Thames and Hudson. 1978.

DAMES, Michael. *"The Silbury Treasure"*. Thames and Hudson. 1976.

DAMES, Michael. *"The Avebury Cycle"*. Thames and Hudson. 1977.

DAVID-NEEL, Alexandra. *"Magic and Mystery in Tibet"*. Mandala. 1965.

DE SANTILLANA, Georgio. "*Hamlet's Mill*" Nonpareil
Books.Godine, Boston. 1977.

EVANS, George Ewart. "*The Horse in the Furrow*". Faber. 1960.

EVANS-WENTZ, W.Y "*The Fairy Faith in Celtic Countries*".
Colin Smythe.1977

EVANS-WENTZ, W.Y "*The Tibetan Book of the Dead*". OUP.
1980.

FENTON, Alexander. "*The Island Blackhouse*". Edinburgh
HMSO. 1978.

FRAZER, J.G. "*The Golden Bough*". Macmillan. 1922.

GALFORD, Ellen. "*The Fires of Bride*". The Women's Press.
1986.

GLOB, P.V. "*The Bog People*". Paladin. 1971.

GORDON, Seton. "*The Immortal Isles*". Williams and Northgate.
1926.

GRAVES, Robert. "*The White Goddess*". Faber and Faber. 1961.

GREGORY, Lady, "*Cuchulain of Muirthemne*". Colin Smythe.
1902/ 1970.

GRIAN, Sinead Sula. "*Brighde, Goddess of Fire*". Brighde's Fire.
1985.

GRIFFIN, Susan "*Woman and Nature*". The Women's Press.
1978.

HADINGHAM, Evan. "*Ancient Carvings in Britain*". Garnstone
Press. 1974.

HEDGES, John W. "*Tomb of the Eagles*". John Murray. 1984.

HESELTON, Philip. "*The Elements of Earth Mysteries*". Element.
1991.

HESELTON, Philip. "*The Secret Places of the Goddess*". Capall
Bann. 1995.

HORWOOD, William. "*Callanish*". Penguin. 1985.

INCH, Sally. "*Birthrights*". Hutchinson. 1982.

JONES, Kathy. "*Spinning the Wheel of Ana*". Ariadne
Publications. 1994.

LIEDLOFF, Jean. "*The Continuum Concept*". Futura. 1975.

MALTWOOD, K.E. "*A Guide to Glastonbury's Temple of the
Stars*". James Clarke and Co. 1964.

MARIECHILD, Diane "*Mother Wit*". The Crossing Press. 1981.

MARTIN, Martin. "*A Description of The Western Isles of
Scotland. 1698*". Birlinn. 1994.

McLUHAN, T.C. (Compiler). *"Touch the Earth"*. Abacus. 1973.
MICHELL, John. *"The View Over Atlantis"*. Abacus. 1973.
NORBU, Namkhai. *"The Crystal and the Way of Light"*. Routledge and Kegan Paul. 1986.
PEARSON, Michael R.R. *"Fisher-Gansey Patterns of Scotland and the Scottish Fleet"*. Esteem Press 1980.
POTTER, Chesca. *"Mysterious Kings Cross"*. Mandrake. 1990.
ROBSON, Michael. *"A Desert Place in the Sea"*. Comunn Eachdraidh Nis. 1997.
SHARKEY, John & PAYNE, Keith. *"The Road Through the Isles"*. Wildwood. 1986.
SINCLAIR, Iain. *"Lud Heat"*. Vintage. 1995.
SINCLAIR-WOOD, Lynne, *"Creating Form From the Mist - The Wisdom of Women in Celtic Myth and Culture"*, Capall Bann Publishing, 1999
SJÖÖ, Monica. *"New Age and Armageddon"*. The Women's Press. 1992.
SJÖÖ, Monica.and MOR, Barbara *"The Great Cosmic Mother"* Harper Row. 1987.
STARHAWK. *"The Spiral Dance"*. Harper & Row. 1979.
STARHAWK. *"Dreaming the Dark"*. Beacon Press. 1982.
STRAFFON, Cheryl. *"The Earth Goddess"*. Cassel. 1997.
SWIRE, Otta F. *"The Outer Hebrides and Their Legends"*. Oliver & Boyd. 1966.
TENZIN-DOLMA, Lisa. *"Swimming With Dolphins"*. Quantum. 1997.
THOM, A. *"Megalithic Lunar Observatories"*. OUP. 1971.
THOMPSON, Gladys. *"Patterns for Guernseys, Jerseys & Arans"*. Dover. 1979.
TOYNE, Phillip. VACHON,Daniel. *"Growing Up The Country"* McPhee Gribble/Penguin 1984
VERNY, Dr.Thomas & KELLY, John. *"The Secret Life of the Unborn Child"*. Sphere. 1982.
WATKINS, Alfred. *"The Old Straight Track"*. Abacus. 1974.
WATKINS, Alfred. *"The Ley Hunter's Manual"*. Pentacle. 1977.
WILLIAMSON, Robin. *"Five Denials on Merlin's Grave"*. Pig's Whisker Music. 1979.

Oh, and there are so many more......

FREE DETAILED CATALOGUE

Capall Bann is owned and run by people actively involved in many of the areas in which we publish. A detailed illustrated catalogue is available on request, SAE or International Postal Coupon appreciated. **Titles can be ordered direct from Capall Bann, post free in the UK** (cheque or PO with order) or from good bookshops and specialist outlets.

Do contact us for details on the latest releases at: **Capall Bann Publishing, Freshfields, Chieveley, Berks, RG20 8TF.** Titles include:

A Breath Behind Time, Terri Hector
Angels and Goddesses - Celtic Christianity & Paganism, M. Howard
Arthur - The Legend Unveiled, C Johnson & E Lung
Auguries and Omens - The Magical Lore of Birds, Yvonne Aburrow
Asyniur - Womens Mysteries in the Northern Tradition, S McGrath
Between Earth and Sky, Julia Day
Book of the Veil , Peter Paddon
Caer Sidhe - Celtic Astrology and Astronomy, Vol 1, Michael Bayley
Call of the Horned Piper, Nigel Jackson
Cat's Company, Ann Walker
Celtic Faery Shamanism, Catrin James
Celtic Faery Shamanism - The Wisdom of the Otherworld, Catrin James
Celtic Lore & Druidic Ritual, Rhiannon Ryall
Celtic Sacifice - Pre Christian Ritual & Religion, Marion Pearce
Celtic Saints and the Glastonbury Zodiac, Mary Caine
Circle and the Square, Jack Gale
Compleat Vampyre - The Vampyre Shaman, Nigel Jackson
Creating Form From the Mist - The Wisdom of Women in Celtic Myth and
    Culture, Lynne Sinclair-Wood
Crystal Clear - A Guide to Quartz Crystal, Jennifer Dent
Crystal Doorways, Simon & Sue Lilly
Crossing the Borderlines - Guising, Masking & Ritual Animal Disguise in the
    European Tradition, Nigel Pennick
Dragons of the West, Nigel Pennick
Earth Dance - A Year of Pagan Rituals, Jan Brodie
Earth Harmony - Places of Power, Holiness & Healing, Nigel Pennick
Earth Magic, Margaret McArthur
Eildon Tree (The) Romany Language & Lore, Michael Hoadley
Enchanted Forest - The Magical Lore of Trees, Yvonne Aburrow
Eternal Priestess, Sage Weston
Eternally Yours Faithfully, Roy Radford & Evelyn Gregory

Everything You Always Wanted To Know About Your Body, But So Far
  Nobody's Been Able To Tell You, Chris Thomas & D Baker
Face of the Deep - Healing Body & Soul, Penny Allen
Fairies in the Irish Tradition, Molly Gowen
Familiars - Animal Powers of Britain, Anna Franklin
Fool's First Steps, (The) Chris Thomas
Forest Paths - Tree Divination, Brian Harrison, Ill. S. Rouse
From Past to Future Life, Dr Roger Webber
Gardening For Wildlife Ron Wilson
God Year, The, Nigel Pennick & Helen Field
Goddess on the Cross, Dr George Young
Handbook For Pagan Healers, Liz Joan
Handbook of Fairies, Ronan Coghlan
Healing Book, The, Chris Thomas and Diane Baker
Healing Homes, Jennifer Dent
Healing Journeys, Paul Williamson
Healing Stones, Sue Philips
Herb Craft - Shamanic & Ritual Use of Herbs, Lavender & Franklin
In Search of Herne the Hunter, Eric Fitch
Intuitive Journey, Ann Walker Isis - African Queen, Akkadia Ford
Journey Home, The, Chris Thomas
Language of the Psycards, Berenice
Legend of Robin Hood, The, Richard Rutherford-Moore
Lid Off the Cauldron, Patricia Crowther
Light From the Shadows - Modern Traditional Witchcraft, Gwyn
Living Tarot, Ann Walker
Lore of the Sacred Horse, Marion Davies
Lost Lands & Sunken Cities (2nd ed.), Nigel Pennick
Magic of Herbs - A Complete Home Herbal, Rhiannon Ryall
Magical Guardians - Exploring the Spirit and Nature of Trees, Philip Heselton
Magical History of the Horse, Janet Farrar & Virginia Russell
Magical Lore of Animals, Yvonne Aburrow
Magical Lore of Cats, Marion Davies
Magical Lore of Herbs, Marion Davies
Magick Without Peers, Ariadne Rainbird & David Rankine
Masks of Misrule - Horned God & His Cult in Europe, Nigel Jackson
Medicine For The Coming Age, Lisa Sand MD
Medium Rare - Reminiscences of a Clairvoyant, Muriel Renard
Mind Massage - 60 Creative Visualisations, Marlene Maundrill
Mirrors of Magic - Evoking the Spirit of the Dewponds, P Heselton
Moon Mysteries, Jan Brodie
Mysteries of the Runes, Michael Howard
New Celtic Oracle The, Nigel Pennick & Nigel Jackson
Pagan Feasts - Seasonal Food for the 8 Festivals, Franklin & Phillips
Patchwork of Magic - Living in a Pagan World, Julia Day
Pathworking - A Practical Book of Guided Meditations, Pete Jennings

FREE detailed catalogue and FREE 'Inspiration' magazine
Contact: Capall Bann Publishing, Freshfields, Chieveley, Berks, RG20 8TF